Not My Little Joseph

Danny Fenn

Published by New Generation Publishing in 2024

Copyright © Danny Fenn 2024

First Edition

ISBN   978-1-83563-192-8

www.newgeneration-publishing.com
New Generation Publishing

The Book Challenge

WHAT'S YOUR STORY?

This book has been supported by
The London Borough of Barking and Dagenham
Library Service - Pen to Print Creative Writing
Programme.
Pen to Print is funded by Arts Council, England
as a National Portfolio Organisation.

Pen to Print

WHAT'S YOUR STORY?

Connect with Pen to Print
Email: pentoprint@lbbd.gov.uk
Web: pentoprint.org

Supported using public funding by
**ARTS COUNCIL
ENGLAND**

Funded by
UK Government

**Barking &
Dagenham**

PROLOGUE

The door was closed quietly by the consultant and I was told to take a seat. My partner Abbie was in the seat next to me gently squeezing my hand, trying to reassure me but in my gut and my heart I knew what was coming. I'm afraid Mr Spencer you have cancer. Bosh. Like a boot in the nuts. All the air seemed to expel from my body till I nearly passed out. Breathe babe says Abbie I'm here, you are going to beat this and I'll be with you every step of the way. I'm only 50 for fuck sake I've got so much more to give, I've got a little granddaughter that don't even know me or how much I love her and how much love I have to give. This ain't my time. How did a decent hard working bloke end up here? Well being honest I ain't always been a decent hard working bloke, I guess I was a bit of what my late mum would call a little toe rag but what others would quite rightly call a proper wrong'un who always put himself before anyone or anything else.

Let me take your hand on a little journey . . .

EARLY YEARS

I was born at the arse end of the 1960s to a doting mum and a drunken vicious father who thank fuck I never really knew as he battered the daylights out of my mum and I am reliably informed tried to clout me round the head with a hot iron because my mum hadn't done his Sunday dinner to his liking. Luckily my mum somehow managed to get him out of our lives not long after. I was a spoilt child being the only boy with five big sisters who all doted on me and looked after me, for which only now as I am older and wiser and have no drugs or chemicals in my body do I appreciate and understand.

I was sent off to infant school and immediately threw a wobbler on the first day, launching my proverbial toys out of the pram after being told off for not knowing the words to All Things Bright and Beautiful and calling the teacher an old bag. Nowadays that wouldn't get any response but early 70s that was an absolute no no. So my schooling didn't start very well and sadly never really improved from that day onwards. I recall in junior school at maybe 7 or 8 years old getting the cane for the very first time and looking round at the rest of the class and thinking don't let them see you cry, Joe, don't let them see you cry.

Now I'd like to say this was the start of a hard man in the making and that I'd go on to be a cross between Ray Winstone in Scum and a future character that would appear on an episode of Danny Dyers deadliest men. But as I said earlier I grew up surrounded by women and burst into tears, and did what I had always done. I bolted out the door out of the school gate and ran home to mum.

So began a life of me manipulating my mum into always believing her little Joseph would never do wrong and it was always someone else's fault. I hated school. I now understand that's because I couldn't control the teachers as

I could control things at home. At school I was just a number and wasn't the centre of the teacher's universe as I fully expected to be. I drifted through junior school with just a handful of friends but mainly I was a loner.

My senior school years were a mish mash of suspensions, detentions, expulsions and truants. We knew by sight and name all the local truant officers and they knew us so it was an ongoing battle of wits. We would go into school, get a mark then dive out the gates and get up to mischief. Aged about 16 a friend had moved to Devon and a car load of us were invited down there for a few days. We had an older mate who had a nice motor and was prepared to drive us all down there but the problem was blagging the time off school. So we all forged fake notes then got our mate the driver John to ring all our parents saying we were going camping as part of a school trip. Somehow, we all pulled it off.

Being a young lad I looked at the A to Z and saw Devon on the map and thought it looked close, but fuck me the drive seemed to take forever. Finally, we arrive and fall out of the motor on the outskirts and walk in an electrical showroom and the bloke peers out from the back of the shop and says in a solid South West accent I'll be with you in a couple of minutes' lads, I'm just finishing my lunch. Our instant response was by eck lads fill yer boots. We filled up the motor with tvs and early top loader video recorders and were gone. Next we walked into a place that sold curtains and bedding all crushed velvet shit. We were running out of room in the fuckin car. It was unreal. The whole place seemed to be oblivious.

We finally arrived at our mates and he was working in a garage where stolen cars were brought in and the vins replaced - called ringing. He was earning a fortune down there. It was a proper eye opener. We plan to go out for a drink that night in the little town he lives in and he warns us if we see the bloke who is known as The Chin don't fuckin look at him he is totally off his rocker. How the fuck will we know we ask? Don't worry you'll know when you see The Chin. So we get changed, head into the little town towards the one pub and as we approach a corner this humongous chin makes its presence known. It seemed to be coming round the corner for ten minutes before the body appeared that it belonged to. Fuckin hells bells says Lunchbox look at the size of that geezer's chin. The Chin - for it was him - just glared at us and turned back the way he had come.

We're sitting in the pub having a jolly old piss up even though we're well under age when all of a sudden the door bursts open and The Chin is ready for war. You cockney bastards have that, he says, and starts swinging a shovel at our heads. He missed my nut by inches and coshed John the driver full on who was out instantly. We're all dashing around the pub trying to escape The Chin's clutches when the governor decides to let his two dogs loose. The Chin is having it with these two Alsatians and we make our escape minus John the driver. John ended up in hospital and we swerved The Chin the rest of the while we were there. He was apparently the result of inbreeding in his family. By the sight of his moosh, it was difficult to argue with.

The next day we decided we would head to a town 12 miles away for a day and night. We ended up stranded after chatting to a few local girls on the beach who were dating a few locals in their early 20s who didn't take kindly to a few out of town teens giving it the big'un, and chased out of town. Somehow we'd got separated and I ended up with my old football companion little Dan in the middle of nowhere as it was getting dark with only a couple of quid to get back to where we were staying.

Me and Dan had travelled up and down the country following our local team for years. He was known as little Dan as his dad was Big Dan, a truly lovely bloke. John was still out of action due to The Chin's shovel so we had to find a phone box and call a cab. The cab turns up and we tell him where we're going and he informs us that it's 12 pounds to which we tell him we'll pay when we get there. But this bloke has more than likely been stitched up by runners many times and weren't having any of it. Pay first or no lift he tells us. We only have 6 quid between us. He says that'll do. We think result but he gets half way, turfs us out, points and says it's about 4 or five miles just keep going down the lane.

Bastard.

It was dark, we had the moors all round us and we were shitting ourselves. No street lights, nothing. I'd like to say me and Dan were like a pair of marines on a mission but that would be a load of bollocks. We were bricking it big time. Every little noise we were grabbing each other's arms with girly squeals of what the fucks that. Plus, we had the stories we'd been told by our mate who lives there about people who'd escaped from Dartmoor nick and roamed and lived wild in the moors. Five miles of pure fuckin terror which we never confessed to any of our mates about.

Next day and night we headed to Plymouth and had all taken magic mushrooms in a massive brew. We picked them as they grew near the gaff we were staying. They were all over the field and though we were saving them to brew up we were also eating them as we walked the field, just picking them and scoffing. Bearing in mind there was all sorts of horse shit in the fields and our only method of knowing what was edible and what was poisonous was Dee. He seemed to have an inbuilt knowledge of every little fungus in the ground. He'd say don't touch that one, then pick another and just eat it. Looking back, it's so stupidly dangerous what we were doing but as Forest Gump's mum so rightly said, stupid is as stupid does.

We arrive in Plymouth and all split in different directions and me and Dee end up watching a Sylvester Stallone film in the cinema tripping on magic mushrooms. We get thrown out the movies and are just walking about when we get into an argument with some big fella. Smack! He cracks Dee on the chin but somehow Dee don't go down. Due to tripping we both react in a way that endeared us to the bloke. Lovely punch mate, says Dee. And I have to agree and congratulate the bloke on the disguise of his right cross. We start waffling away and end up going in a pub with the fella and he buys us a drink and turns out he is a soldier and served in The Falklands. We congratulate him on his punch once more then leave him wondering what the fuck these two lads are on.

We're wandering about for a couple of hours and as we're walking across a road, a car reverses into us. We bang on the back of the motor. Oi you prick watch what you're doing. A big old lump of a geezer gets out and squares up to us and I'm thinking shit this lump is going to put us both on our arse. Then just as he's about to chin us from nowhere he's decked by our courageous soldier mate. Fuckin hell where you come from we say. He just happened to be walking along. Right place right time. He tells us to get back to where we were staying as it's getting late and it's a dangerous place for young uns. We heed his advice and scoot off out of there.

When we arrived back home, John the driver was still knocked up in hospital, and has life changing effects with headaches etc. and has never been able to hold a job down since due to panic attacks. We sold all our electrical and crushed velvet goodies to the older lot in The Partridge and informed all the local tea leaves how backwards Devon was as far as security in the shops.

A few months later a few of them jumped on a coach to Exeter then to Devon to earn a few quid and all ended up getting nicked. It seems we had woken the place up and security was beefed up and they all got caught, nicked and back and forwards to court. You have to bear in mind I was still a young lad at this time and still supposed to be at school. I was suspended a couple of times for being unruly in the class and then finally expelled. I somehow convinced my dear mum yet again it was all a misunderstanding and she arranged a meeting with the headmaster. She persuaded him to give me another chance but me being me it lasted no more than a couple of weeks.

I wasn't violent just disruptive to the other kids and was messing up their chances of learning by being, to put it truthfully, a grade one prick. I now know I just wanted to get attention but went about it in the wrong way. I enjoyed PE and English and drama and that was it. I was creative with my writing but it wasn't encouraged so that just slipped by and I loved drama but got stick off me mates for doing it so rather than being my own person I knocked that on the head as well.

I was then expelled for good and my dear old mum had to find another school that would take me. The only one that was prepared to give me a chance was about five miles away and I would have to jump on a train and bus, or walk.

The first day there I was full of trepidation as it was out of my safety area. I knew no-one and was known as a trouble maker so was going to be a target for the school hard nuts. The school consisted of two buildings about half a mile apart and the first person I spoke to informed me how easy it was to duck out of lessons between the two buildings. So for my whole year there I barely managed to complete a full day.

When it was time for the CSE exams I bunked off those as well for good measure. I keep saying it, but what an absolute bell-end I was. My mum would send me off for the exams with high expectations and I would pretend to go in for the exam and piss off elsewhere. She kept asking me when we were going to get my results and I kept putting it off till she got a letter asking why I hadn't attended. Again I convinced her it was all a mistake and it was the schooling system that had messed up not her little Joseph.

She truly believed I was destined to be a carpenter.

I was, and still am, useless at any type of DIY but in the third year we had a woodwork exam and had three one hour lessons to make either a car or a boat. Now I am useless with any tool, if you give me a hammer and nail you will need to ring 999 because I will end up smashing the nail through my hand and pinning myself to the wall. Even now if there is something needs doing at home and I tell Abbie I'm going to put a shelf up or something she'll say don't you dare and hide the tools.

Anyhow during this exam, it was coming near to the end of the final lesson and all I had was the same square piece of wood we were given at the start. I noticed a lad Andrew had created a top little car with working wheels, steering wheel, the lot. So when he put it down and turned his back I did what any like-minded horrible little bastard would and grabbed it and left my block on his work bench. I quickly planed off his name and replaced it with J. Spencer.

There was a big fuss when Andrew was searching for his masterpiece. The teacher knew I was shit at woodwork but couldn't prove otherwise so had to accept that it was mine. I got great marks for my car and poor Andrew didn't have time to do another and flopped. When I presented mum with my great piece of work she was overjoyed. She kept that car till her final day on earth and everyone who came into her front room she would tell them her little Joseph should have been a chippie, look at the car he made at school. I never had the heart to tell her the truth and still have the car. To Andrews credit it still steers perfectly.

I do hope he ended up fulfilling his potential.

Me, I left school a lying manipulative little shit.

GLUE SNIFFING, AMONG OTHER THINGS . . .

I was probably first year senior school, so about 12 years old, when I first sniffed glue. It was over a place known locally to us in our little patch of London/Essex as the fox's den where all the older locals would go to drink, smoke and sniff. They didn't particularly want us younger kids there but as soon as they realised how good me and my mates were at shop lifting they soon accepted us with open arms and glue bags aplenty.

The glue of choice was either Fix O Fix or Evo Stik. Both were literally mind blowing and mind altering. We were in our own little world, the train lines only 20 yards in front of us and at times we would just wander onto the tracks. How none of us were ever killed by a train is a miracle? I recall one time a young lad by the name of Jay fell on the lines and was picked up just before being splattered. But being young and totally out of our heads we all just laughed it off.

Another time a mate was convinced all his teeth had fallen out and a lad called Shaun spent an hour rummaging about looking for these teeth in a fox's den. We held him by his feet and like a Jack Russel he had his top half down the den searching for the teeth.

Another occasion a local skinhead who was renowned as a local nutter/hard nut, Patsy Brooker, was walking towards me and a mate down the local subway that went under the old A13 road and we spotted that Patsy had a glue bag that he was sniffing from inside his Crombie overcoat. Unbeknown to me and my mate Alfie, he was also carrying a small axe down one sleeve of said Crombie and when we walked up to him and dared to ask him if he would mind sharing his glue bag with us he proceeded to pull out the axe and charged us.

I may not have been much good at anything at school but I did always excel at sports and could proper have it on me toes when necessary and this was definitely one of those occasions.

As a side note, years later Patsy was on a LSD trip one day on the roof of a four storey building and in his spaced out mind the ground was just a small step away. Sadly, for Patsy, it wasn't. He lived to tell the tale. A couple of years after, Patsy used to come and buy his puff off me in The Partridge. I often thought maybe I'll remind him of the axe incident but he'd calmed down now he smoked dope instead of sniffing glue, so I thought it prudent to keep schtum as he might have gone elsewhere for his gear and he had become a good customer of mine. Anyway, what's a little axe attack between friends.

The problem with sniffing glue was trying to get it off your breath before going home as the smell stayed for hours. I remember being told by someone that puddle water would remove the smell so I actually got on my hands and knees, lapping up the rain water. Funnily enough, it never worked. As well as the smell on me breath, after a while I began to develop sores from the bag around my mouth.

I recall the woodwork teacher in school class was a little old bald bloke called Mr Marshall. He would sign us all in then half a dozen of us would nick the glue and run off to the school field, sniff the glue then come staggering back hallucinating. The poor bloke never had a clue where all his pupils were vanishing to along with the glue. At one point when it rained a few of us literally crawled into the underneath of one of the work benches to get our daily sniff rather than leaving the comfort and warmth of the classroom.

From glue we progressed to tins of gas. Nothing I'm proud of but I cannot change things I've done. I can only learn from my mistakes. I often wonder what caused me to constantly seek a buzz to take me away from reality as I was loved by my family but it seemed the only time I was happy was when I was stoned or creating and causing trouble for myself and those around me. Gas was similar to glue in that it completely fried the brain and was a mental buzz. I now understand how dangerous it was each and every time we popped the lid off a tin and headed off over the back of the local church into a world of hallucinations and sheer madness.

The Old Bill by then were a permanent thorn in our side as for some reason they didn't like the fact that we were going out thieving from shops and sniffing tins of gas behind the church, and generally giving the local residents a bit of a nightmare. We used to dig holes in the uneven surface behind the church and fill it with broken bottles and then wait for the Old Bill to turn up and give them the wanker sign and shout ACAB (all coppers are bastards) and for some odd reason this would send them wild and they would come steaming round the back of the church before falling arse over tit into our little Old Bill traps.

Brutal some may say but when they did get hold of us they more than made up for it with fists, boots and truncheons. There was an unwritten code that both us and the Old Bill seemed to abide by where we lived outside the law and knew the risks we took. Same with the Old Bill if they caught us we were more than likely gonna get a clump or three. Swings and roundabouts, I suppose.

There was some poor bloke lived behind the church who due to having a moustache was christened Hitler by every kid and teenager within a five-mile radius. He took absolute dogs abuse day in day out from one group of kids to the next. His windows were smashed on a regular basis with snooker balls from the local youth club. He quite rightly took to defending himself and his property with a catapult firing lead bearings at us and also began to use his car, a lovely Cortina mark 3, as a retaliatory weapon.

I recall one time sprinting full pelt down the road, Hitler in hot pursuit driving up on the pavement to get his revenge on one of the little shits that had made his life a misery by squashing me with his lovely Mark 3. As I said earlier, though, I was always good at PE and sports if nothing else and at the last second hurdled a fence and Hitler proceeded to plough into a neighbouring wall. He ended up getting nicked at the scene and not long after he moved away. A couple of years later a mate who lived a fair few miles away mentioned in school guess who's moved in next door to me? Hitler, the poor sod. So, being the horrible little bastards that we were, off we trooped to give him some more stick.

I hope he eventually found some peace and as I keep saying it's not something I'm proud of, what seemed to us as a bit of a laugh made some poor man's life hell, I am honestly ashamed of the way we treated him.

I would guess I sniffed glue more days than I didn't for about two years. God knows how we survived with our brains still intact. At one point I remember not having any money for glue so decided to syphon some petrol from a car and sniff that instead. It all went well till I put the petrol in a little crisp bag and blew and then inhaled and swallowed the fuel. I was shitting myself convinced if someone lit up a fag near me I would explode. I eventually stuck my fingers down my throat and puked it all up, again, and got away with another one.

SMOKING DOPE AND TRIPPING

Then one day when I was about 14 and a couple of older fellas had a bit of puff - or red leb to call it by its proper name - and offered us a little pull on the joint. Now smoking dope in 2022 is nothing like it was back in the early to mid-80s. It was nowhere near as strong as it is now but if you were caught with even a joint you would end up with a charge sheet and a court case and your name would be shamed in the local paper for every man and his dog to see.

Thing is I absolutely loved the feeling of smoking dope. It was nothing like the shit I was sniffing before i.e. glue, gas or Typex thinners. It was much gentler and just seemed to make me giggle for a while and appreciate chocolate and music like never before. For the next 20 years' puff became what I thought was my drug of choice whereas looking back free from all chemicals as I am now, I know it had a serious hold over me. Much as we all said this would be it and we would never touch anything stronger, sadly that wasn't the case. I have since had to watch so many good friends slip into that never ending cycle of getting clean then drifting back into the drug lifestyle, a lot heavier than just smoking a joint.

Back then though all that seemed impossible as we all knew what we were doing and could easily control ourselves. Or so we thought. It was not long after this that I took my first acid LSD tablet. There was a local bloke known as Tricky Dicky who seemed to have a never ending supply of every Illegal substance on the market. We were only about 14 or perhaps 15 so someone older had to knock at Tricky Dicky's door and buy me and my mate Neil an acid each.

Myself and Neil - known by all and sundry as Dee - became very close for a number of years. We still occasionally chat but Dee somehow manages to still live like he did when he was a teenager. Even though he's now into his mid-50s he must have more chemicals in his body than a small pharmacy. He'll never just have one acid, he'll pop a few, as well as drop an ecstasy, smoke untold amounts of skunk and all along with a bottle of JD and still hold a fully coherent conversation. I have no idea how he does it but he's a proper decent bloke. He's got one of those infectious laughs that once he starts everyone else will be in hysterics with him.

So me and Neil were bunking off school. It was about 10 in the morning and popped the acid we had from Tricky Dicky's. By about half 10 we were about to go and throw a brick through Tricky's window as the acid was shit. On the way we both start laughing then wallop the trip came on. Acid really is a total mind fuck of a drug. Everything just seems to come alive. We ended up knocking on Trick's door totally off our heads begging for more. He didn't have a clue who we were and ended up chasing us away from his house as we were making such a row and drawing attention to the fact he was dealing.

A few years later I began selling for Tricky Dicky in my local boozer, *The Partridge*, and got on well with him. He would get raided on a regular basis. The Old Bill would always find something and he'd do a 6-month stretch then be straight out and start dealing again. I suppose it was what he knew so he just cracked on with it, as so many do. *The Partridge* was an old style local boozer where everyone knew everyone else. If you were a stranger, mind, it was a menacing looking establishment and had a bad name. The only strangers who were welcome were those coming in to purchase pharmaceuticals or knocked off goods. It was rightfully known as, among other names as *The Flying Bottle*, *The Gaping Wound*, and *The Dentist*. *The Dentist* because if you couldn't get an appointment at the official practitioner there was always someone willing to knock your tooth out free of charge.

It was also known as *The Pharmacy* - for obvious reasons.

Looking back with hindsight it was a dangerous place and there was these sort of rites of passage to gain an honorary membership. At first you would walk by as a kid and hear the shouting and the music from inside and see the kids left outside by their parents with a bag of crisps and fizzy drink, while hearing the sounds of bottles and glasses smashing. Then you'd get to an age of about 16 or 17 and venture in the door for the first time and with trepidation you'd walk towards the bar with all eyes on ya waiting for an elder who would have seen you out and about to give you a nod. Next step would be trying to get served when you are blatantly too young and getting short shrift from the barmaids. Then you would progress to getting served with your mates until you became part of the established crowd.

There was a sort of hierarchy of the older blokes in their 60s - war babies who'd known proper hard times - who had seen it and done it all by the time I was finding my feet. Then there were the blokes in their 40s and 30s who we would look up to, then you would have those in their 20s and us in our teens. Each generation feels that they know more and are more clued up than the last but when it all comes down to it we were all from working class families just trying to enjoy life. There was a fight every night which would usually end up outside and the police being called. The next day the two antagonists would be sitting laughing and joking and sharing a beer and all was forgotten. On a Sunday there would be roast potatoes put on the bar with peanuts and a few plates of crisps, There were probably pubs very much like *The Partridge* in towns up and down the country at the time, though now they are sadly disappearing and turning into the more family orientated pub/restaurant places. Which I much prefer now, funnily enough. I don't want to be sitting looking over my shoulder every time the door opens.

On a Sunday afternoon there would be a couple of strippers on the stage doing a saucy dance and a few fellas would get a bit carried away but the ladies knew how to look after themselves and the blokes would soon be put in their place. Tuesday night was the so called grab a granny night though the majority of the females who turned up were no older than 40 and just out for a good night.

Back to the LSD

I had many great times on acid and on one heavy trip a mate just made a passing remark of don't that lamppost look sad? Now in my freaked out acid addled mind I glanced at the lamppost and saw that unlike all the other posts in the street it didn't have a top above the actual light and I said yeah poor fucker is proper on a downer. By now my mates had all given up on me and fucked off and left me in the company of the streetlights. But more importantly, my new sad friend.

Now I could fully empathise with this piece of street furniture as I always felt as if I never quite fit in although I was obviously the same as everyone else but always seemed slightly different which in my mind created a bond with Mr Lamppost here. I explained how, like him, how my top was a wee bit different to everyone else and I always searched for reassurance etc. I found the lamppost totally unjudgemental - unlike many people I had encountered in my short time on earth. I like to feel I gave him (maybe I am assuming the gender of the lamppost community and it was a female, and I never asked for their name) a spiritual lift while they were down in the dumps. I truly hope that I gave some comfort and much needed love to him/her and if they are still about I hope not too many dogs have cocked their legs and had a piss up my old pal.

That night I spent a good few hours with my mates the lampposts. Many people walked past giving this mad looking young bloke a wide berth. But who were they to judge me as the local psychiatrists had tried to?

There was a time, you see, when I was maybe 11 or 12 years old when I was sent to a place called River brook Hall. Nowadays people would probably go there without being judged by others but back then it was seen as a sign you were a nutter. I sat with what I gather were some kind of child psychiatrists once or twice a week for a year or so. They would produce cards and tell me to tell them the first thing that came into my head when they turned each card for me to view. Now to me each picture just resembled a messy blob which is how I referred to them. But they weren't happy with that answer and told me maybe one resembled a fish so I agreed that yes it looked like a fish.

The next one looked like a messy blob which I told them but they told me maybe it looked like a cloud so I agreed. This just went on and on with me agreeing with whatever I was told I was meant to be seeing in the messy blobs. So each week I would say the same thing that I could see in these cards repeating from memory what I was told to see.

One very long wasted year I spent going back and forth to River brook but I did discover a cupboard on the stairwell that was packed out with electric fans, brand new in boxes of which I would help myself to once every couple of weeks and sell for a tenner each till they realised the fans were slowly diminishing in number and I was caught red handed by one of the shrinks. I did my usual of throwing a wobbler, kicking him in the shins and running away. The police got involved and somehow between my lovely mum and the psychiatrists they agreed to not press any charges. Another occasion for me to convince my doting mum it was all a mistake and the stars aligned in the wrong way and yes, she would tell them. Not my little Joseph.

The downside of this was that other locals got to hear about it. It wasn't the fact that I was thieving or that I had kicked the bloke between the legs that I was embarrassed about, it was the fact it came out I was seeing psychiatrists and suddenly I was considered a nutter. This had its downside but also some good points as being considered a nutter made a large amount of other kids who would otherwise have bullied me wary of me. When they eventually had enough of me at River brook there was no real diagnosis, I was apparently just a naughty young lad seeking attention? Personally I feel I was a little shit who always wanted what wasn't mine and who was always looking for an escape from reality.

One time we were down London, a big crowd off us all tripping out of our nuts. Some bloke was sitting on a bench opposite the Thames along the Embankment with a street light flickering above him, a bottle of spirits in a brown paper bag in his hand staring off into space as still as the night. He looked like a painting and we all came to the conclusion in our stoned minds that he wasn't real and was just a hallucination. A mate convinced me to go over and touch him which being the gullible twat I am I did. Just as I touched him he jumped towards me and projectile vomited all over me and just keeled over and had a seizure at my feet. This was before mobile phones so we had to bolt to find a phone box to call an ambulance while all the time being spaced out on acid.

We ended up outside Buckingham Palace shouting at the top of our voices and one mate Terry was convinced he was in a swimming pool and was laying there doing the front crawl outside her majesty's humble abode. Suddenly from nowhere Old Bill were swarming all round us due to our noise within the proximity of the palace. They were trying to question us but anyone who has ever done acid will know everything becomes funny and we just kept laughing at their questions.

We managed to convince them that we were just naïve youngsters who had shared a bottle of vodka. Then they spotted our man Terry now doing his very best backstroke before slamming into the palace gates doing a very realistic swimming turn and kick. What's he doing? a copper asked. In unison all of us just said he's fuckin swimming what's it look like he's fuckin doing? That was enough for them and we were lobbed in the Old Bill cars and spent several hours tripping in police cells. All the while I'm covered in some pissheads puke.

Lovely.

Another time I remember sitting having to eat a dinner halfway through an acid trip at the table with my mum and step dad and I was convinced that I could drink the food. Bearing in mind it was roast beef and potatoes that I was trying to actually drink instead of chewing it was never going to end well. My poor mum was horrified having to constantly do the Heimlich manoeuvre on her precious son till it all came up. My stepdad was telling her it's because I was on drugs but I somehow managed to convince her I was just drunk. I like to believe she believed that, anyway.

LSD is a seriously dangerous drug to mess about with. It can have life changing effects on your mind if you have a bad trip - of which I did a few times. A particular time that comes to mind I was somewhere up London with half a dozen mates all wandering around Leicester square off our faces and everywhere we went some bloke would appear. He was dressed in a dog tooth suit and white tie and no matter where we went he would be standing, staring at us from a distance.

At first it was just a laugh with us going there's that bloke again. We'd be getting on night buses and getting off in other parts of the city and he would be standing there when we turned a corner. To this day I have no idea what the fuck he was up to but he freaked us all out big time. So we went from London to the outskirts and a lake where things didn't improve for our acid frazzled brains. We had to cross a railway bridge to get to the lake and some bastard had painted an illuminous devil on the bridge which took us about an hour to finally get passed. Fuckin terrifying, it was.

Then as we're trying to relax wallop a massive flash lights up the sky. Some strange little hobbit type bloke appears and starts taking photos of us with an old Kodak style camera offering us to go with him back to a flat. When you are on that shit it really does have an effect but yeah fuck right off, mate.

As for coke I always saw it as speed /sulphate but just more expensive. It was never my cup of tea really and it's mental how it has swept the country big time and now it's even swabbed in the toilets in Parliament by all accounts. Madness, all doing lines off filthy bog systems but it has really exploded as the drug of choice among all classes. Now you will see people on spice literally walking and acting like zombies. It's a synthetic version similar to the main ingredient in cannabis that gives off the buzz of puff but on a grander scale and I have witnessed those on the gear completely zoned out. It is a frightening drug with many variants and madly is only a class B drug?

Work that one out.

DRINK

As I said earlier, my dad was an alcoholic and I just seemed to take to drink like a seasoned boozer. From about 13 I was regularly emptying my stepdad's drinks cabinet of anything that would get me pissed. I would fill up the vodka and Bacardi bottles with water to disguise the fact I had been necking it. But then one day he came home early from work seeing me bunking school pissed as a newt and said to my mum I'm going to teach him a lesson. He then made me drink what he thought was a bottle of vodka but was really water as I'd already caned it. When my poor mum saw how easily I drank the so-called vodka she broke down in tears at the thought her darling boy was such a heavy drinker, which, sadly. I was.

Back in the 80s when I was old enough - or at least looked old enough to get served in pubs I would be out shoplifting first thing in the morning getting enough for an eighth of dope and an afternoon's drinking. It was easy back then to walk in a shop, sneak into the window display and bowl off with a television or video recorder for a quick sale and a nice easy mornings graft.

One time a mate of mine, Noel, asked me if I fancied a job for a few months in a well-known clothes store. I jumped at the opportunity to fill my boots. I'd been getting in there before I got a job there ripping the alarms off the leather jackets. I could get 30/ 40 quid per jacket which was a fair sum back in the 80s/90s. Straight away, as a member of staff, I was put upstairs in the warehouse part entrusted with putting the alarms on the clothes before they went down to the actual shop.

Unbelievable.

I was like a pig in shit.

I swiftly discovered that when I went for lunch I went out the staff entrance at the back. All I had to do was go to the exit, press the buzzer and whoever was nearest the monitor upstairs would release the door. I sussed out some other fella Craig was up for a little earner and said to him I'll chuck you a score a week if each lunch time you stand by the monitor and let me out. He was game so I put one of the leather jackets under my coat, pressed the door buzzer and walked out with it. Simple as that. Then it was just a matter of where to stash it till I finished work later in the day.

The local Barracuda swimming pool was nearby so I walked there, paid 50 pence to spectate then put the leather in one of the lockers with another 50 pence and it was job done. It was easy money. I'd gone from trying to sneak in the shop avoiding staff and store detectives, ripping off the alarms and walking out waiting for the dreaded hand on the shoulder to just strolling out the staff exit.

This for the next 4 months became a regular earner, one leather at lunchtime placed in a locker at the swimming pool then another when we finished work, I would then go back to the Barracuda, pay another 50 pence to spectate, put my key in, bag up the other leather and off I'd go. Sadly, this honest life of working in a store soon finished but it was a pleasure to work for them.

By the age of 16 I was always seen with a bottle of vodka in my hand or a few cans of strong lager. Bearing in mind back then pubs closed at 3pm weekdays would reopen at 5. In the 2 hour gap I would drunkenly go out thieving getting me enough to see me through the night back in the pub. It would eventually get to the stage where I would buy 4 cans on my way home at the end of the night in preparation for the following morning, so I'm guessing even then I was on my way to having quite a heavy drink problem.

Drink mixed with drugs led to me feeling the long arm of the law on a fair few occasions till I ended up in a young offender's establishment. Myself and Dee had got an acid each - the old style Superman ones - and were on our way through some local factories. From nowhere Dee was suddenly riding a motorbike. To this day I have no idea where it came from but there it was, our ride for the day. Dee would walk off - or in this case ride off - with absolutely anything if it weren't nailed down.

As we're walking through the factories we noticed a big stack of boxes sitting on a pallet. Straight away I jump off the back of the bike and try choring a couple of the boxes which turned out to contain blank vhs cassette tapes. Next thing I know some bloke smacks me in the head from behind shouting I'm the assistant manager and this is a citizen's arrest. Then just to add to the bad luck I'm jumped on by a few fellas pinning me down. It turns out they're plain clothes Old Bill and had been following us for a good while. Off we went to the station and next morning we're up in Magistrates court. The Old Bill objected to us getting bail as we were already out on bail on a conspiracy charge.

Now I could leave that there and it makes it look like some elaborate plot to rob the Bank of England when in fact it was nothing of the sort. About a year before 7 of us had bought some mogadons from a few of the local heroin addicts. Mogadons were pills given to the heroin addicts to help them but they used to sell them to us so they could buy themselves a proper fix. Mix mogadons with alcohol, though, and it's a lethal combination. So, being us, that's what we did. Mogadons and alcohol make you honestly believe you're Mike Tyson, totally invincible. We ended up staggering around a shopping centre helping ourselves to cans of beer and bits and pieces from whatever shop took our fancy. But as for it being a conspiracy like the Old Bill said, that couldn't be any further from the truth as we were all totally smashed out of our brains and to conspire you have to plan and we were so smashed we couldn't have planned an orgy in a brothel.

The conspiracy case dragged on for about 3 years before eventually the majority of us were cleared and a couple were found guilty of theft. This was early days of CCTV and we kept bursting out with laughter in the dock watching some of the things we'd done while out of our heads on mogadons and drink. Several times we were rammed 7 of us in the dock that was only meant to hold 2 or 3 at most, stoned and all laughing and acting like knobs. At one point the magistrates were going to do us for contempt of court.

Anyway, bail was refused and being the clever fuckers we were, we still had an acid each and decided to pop them before the Sweat Box arrived to take us to the remand centre. It's called the Sweat Box which has the name because it is full of about 20 individual little hard seats with its own little door which is locked from outside by the screw and you end up sweating your nuts off in there. Big big mistake. Now Dee and his brother Stuart spent their early years in children's homes and had both had the short sharp shock treatment of a detention centre so knew what to expect whereas I had always managed to wriggle out of things, but that was about to change.

Dee shouts grab my shirt don't let go to me and Joe as we're taken into Lambeth Old Bill station where they throw us all in a holding cell, adding and tell anyone who asks you don't smoke. Do what, I've replied, what you mean? Now I'm proper coming up on the acid we took in the Sweat Box and getting the horrors. Everyone and everything becomes a threat and frightens the life out of me.

Where they've put us is the biggest cell you can imagine. A bench is all the way round the edge and about 50 /60 prisoners are all packed in there and charge towards us as the door is slammed shut. I grab onto Dee's shirt like he said and get it in a death like grip as we - along with about half a dozen other newcomers - are welcomed by the mob.

Give us a burn is shouted at me from every direction from menacing looking faces of every description. I didn't even know what a burn was. It turns out quite obviously it's something to smoke. Next thing some big black lad is trying to pull my trainers off my feet. Give me your trainers or I'll give you a dig he screams. I had a pair of Reebok Classics on at the time which were, believe it or not, the height of fashion and one of the best trainers about at the time. I obviously never bought them. I had somehow convinced a member of staff in a sports shop that the pair of trainers I was wearing were new and had ripped but sadly had lost the receipt so could I try on the Reeboks. She got a pair of Reeboks out, I tried them on and did my usual of having it away on my toes in my brand new pair of trainers.

I managed to pull this little stunt for a number of years so always had decent footwear.

Anyway, back to the holding cell. This lovely fella - who I eventually get to know as Scooby and is awaiting extradition to the States - is trying to pull my trainers off my feet. I wouldn't mind but his feet are huge and I was only size 7. Luckily I managed to keep hold of Dee's shirt and sat on the bench, trainers still attached to my feet but still tripping on the acid. Acid can be such a funny drug, but when your mind is not in the right place it can play havoc and cause severe anxiety which was now happening.

The door opens again and a few new recruits are thrown into the lion's den and the mob's attention, thank fuck, are drawn towards these.

We ended up sharing a joint with Scooby and a few of his pals and this slowly but surely started my brain on a comedown from the acid at the same time being in sheer shock at being banged up and on my way to nick.

After about an hour or so a screw opens the door and calls out about ten names - including mine and Dee, Scooby, and another big black lad called Kelly who would play another big part in the story a few months down the line - and tells us we're off to Ashford remand centre.

On the drive to Ashford in a different Sweat Box I remember looking out of the one-way glass at people going about their business just doing normal things, living normal everyday lives and it suddenly really hit home and I admit I sat there and sobbed quietly to myself. I was begging and praying to any God who would listen please, please get me out of this situation and I'll get an honest job, go to church every week and never touch a drug again.

But God was obviously busy that day cos this was real and suddenly the prison walls loomed large as the van stopped at the barrier. The door opened and we were all trooped across the yard to the reception. I was keeping Dee, Scooby and Kelly as close as possible as I was absolutely bricking it.

In we went and first thing that hit me was the smell of piss. I found out after that nearby was where the A wing prisoners emptied their piss pots each day, hence the smell. Then we were all stripped off and a screw had a look and little fiddle up my arse for any drugs or weapons stashed up there. According to those more experienced prisoners the screws were getting a boner while searching our crevices, to which the screws told them to watch their mouths or get a clump.

Next, into the shower - which was freezing cold - before walking out with a little towel wrapped round my waist, where I was introduced to a prisoner who was referred to as Mr T as in the big bloke from The A Team (a big tv series in the 80s). In my opinion, this fella was more like Mr T's much bigger brother. He was built like the proverbial brick shit house and frightened the granny out of me. It was Mr T's job to give us our clothes. He took one look at me and threw me a pair of grey trousers, a faded grey shirt and jumper, a pair of awful shoe/ clodhoppers and a stained pair of white Y fronts. I weren't about to tell Mr T I needed smaller pants so obediently got dressed and ended up with my pants tucked under me armpits, doing a Simon Cowell impression long before he made the look famous. We were then led into a corridor into a mass of voices shouting, screaming and whistling, and the overwhelming smell of piss. I was given a piss pot, a plastic mug and a little jug of water. Luckily for me I was thrown in a cell on E wing with Dee. At least I was with my mate and knew he would look after me.

First thing I noticed as the door slammed shut was a previous inmate had put a crisp bag over the inside of the spy hole. Being a good upstanding citizen I say to Dee shall I take that down we might get in trouble? Dee as always to the point says fuck it we're already in trouble bollocks to em. So I heed his words of wisdom and leave it there.

Dee being Dee, bosh he's out like a light whereas I'm still coming down from the worst trip I'm ever likely to have, laying there half the night worrying and still hoping to God someone somewhere will hear my pleas and get me out of there. I eventually fall into a deep but troubled sleep when next thing I hear is something heavy hitting metal and a voice repeating, "I suppose you think this is funny you little scrote?"

I open my eyes wondering where the fuck I am and get my first glimpse of who I will later learn is known by all the prisoners as well as most other screws as Bronco Billy. Bronco was a screw and a bully and rumour was he was known as Bronco due to the fact that he would ride young vulnerable cons in return for a couple of joints and apparently had once been suspended after a young lad complained but he ended up getting his job back anyway.

Back to the narrative.

I suppose you think it's funny? Bronco looked like a typical sergeant major, resembling Windsor Davis from It Ain't Half Hot Mum. Similar hairstyle, booming voice, barrel chested and very intimidating. What? was my reply to which he pointed to the crisp bag covering the spy hole. Straight away I say I don't know what you're on about it was there when we got here.

He walks over asking Dee the same but Dee ain't having none of it and just tells Bronco to piss off. Typical bully he comes back to me and tells me he's going to be watching me very closely from now on. I think to myself I bet you are you fuckin pervert.

Then it was straight into the breakfast hall packed with hundreds of cons full of noise and threatening faces all posing and trying to look menacing. Still the smell of piss permeated even the bacon we were served up had the smell of strong urine, you could almost taste it. Actually you probably could taste it, but that don't bare thinking about.

I just tried to look down at my food and not make eye contact with anyone as I was truly pooping me pants.

I know this time I'm completely out of my depth.

FOUR WALLS

After breakfast me and Dee were walking back to our cell when we've heard oi oi Dee, Spence oi oi son. Unbelievably it was Dee's older brother Stuart. He came up and said what the fuck you 2 doing here? We briefly explained and he told us he'd just been to the dentist and had a tooth out but would come down to our cell in an hour and have a good old puff, saying all this in front of a screw. I looked at Stuart as if to say Jesus are you mad? But I should've known better. Stuart said I've got the gaff under manners, son.

True to his word an hour or so later our cell door opens and in bowls Stuart, gives us a Roberts Rambler radio with a spare battery, throws me a pack of rizla, a fag and a lump of Moroccan's finest hash and says skin up son.

Now Stuart is worth a book on his own but to cut it short him and Dee grew up in several children's homes before their wonderful nan took them in years later. He is a natural born leader and would have made a great captain in the army. He's the sort of fella you'd want by your side in the trenches, and at that moment the four walls of this gaff seemed like I was in the trenches. God was I was glad to see him. However, I was still getting used to the surroundings so was proper paranoid about rolling a joint and just lying there and smoking knowing a screw could come and open the door at any moment.

As far as I remember the cell had 9 little windows and you could fit your head through the middle one which I did while holding my joint out of the other side window and started to nervously smoke my joint while Stuart and Dee just sprawled out on the 2 bunks with Bob Marley playing soothing sounds from our new Roberts Rambler. As soon as someone smelt my joint from another cell window below I heard oi fella swing me a line and pass me a joint. Stuart jumps up comes over to the window and shouts oi soppy bollocks it's my little brother and his pal in here so shut the fuck up.

Sorry Stuart mucker, comes the instant reply, don't worry mate I'll make sure they're sweet. Simple as that. I knew Stuart quite well but was finding out how much sway he genuinely carried. He went on to explain to me what swing a line was. He proceeded to rip my bed sheet all-round the edge top to bottom, side to side, till we had a long length of material. He then tied my plastic tea mug to one end, put a small ready rolled joint in the cup, covered it with a sock then called down to the fella who had asked me earlier for a joint and said I'm swinging you a joint down. He then swung the long piece of material across to the bloke in the cell below who then passed it to the bloke who received the package. He took the sock off, took the joint out and replaced it with some tobacco which was then swung back up to us. You live and learn every day and it truly is a great way of passing stuff about from cell to cell.

Days turned into weeks and I slowly, with Dee's help, began to adjust to the new surroundings and how things were. One day I had an encounter with a big scouse lad who blatantly robbed me of a book. It was a *Minder* book - as in Arthur Daley and Terry McCann.

Now Scouse was a big old lump and he walked up to me as I was walking down the wing after borrowing the book from Kelly who I'd first met in the holding cell at Lambeth. Scouse sized me up, pushed me into the wall and took the book out of my hand and stared me down waiting to see my reaction. Straight away my arse fell out and I let him just take it and off he swaggered.

I got back to our cell and Dee asked why I looked freaked out so I told him what had happened and he went nuts. Shouting at me Spence what have I told ya don't let no fucker take a liberty or everyone will treat you like a fraggle and take the piss. What was I meant to do? I said, you seen the size of him? Yeah but if you'd just told him bollocks and smacked him at least you'd have stood your ground and wouldn't look like a plum. We're going to have to go and front him out and get it back.

This was all I needed but I knew I had to do it or word would get around and I'd have everyone taking liberties. We stopped in Stu`s cell on the way and told him. He gave me a bollocking but said look Scouse is all mouth I'll come with ya but you're the one that's got to let him know he's taken the piss.

So off we troop. All the while I just want to run and hope the problem will solve itself but I was now slowly understanding that isn't what it was like in the real world.

We walk up and into Scouse's cell. Hello Stu mate, says scouse, then he sees me and thinks little fuckers grassed me up, I could see it in his eyes. Steve says Scouse this is Dee my brother and his Co-D (co-defendant) Spence who is also a good pal of mine and you've proper took the piss. I was then pushed forward and in my bravest Clint Eastwood voice said I want my book back you . . . you've took a proper liberty, fully expecting to get sparked out.

So sorry Spence I didn't know you were Stu's pal. We ended up getting the book back and a joint as an apology and Scouse said any hag on my wing give me a shout and I'll back you up.

Fuck me, I was constantly squirming out of proper dodgy situations and landing on me feet smelling of roses. I've been told as I've got older that I am a lucky bastard who obviously has someone or something looking after me. Scouse did get a little bit of revenge, though, out on the rugby pitch. Dee had a visit off some bird he was sort of seeing at the time and while I was laying in the cell feeling all sorry for myself the door opens and it's the PE screw. He says you fancy a game of football.

Fuck me does Dolly Parton sleep on her back, course I do. So we get down to the freezing cold pitch and there's about 30 of us standing there. We're asked what you want to do rugby or football? Now I weighed about 10 stone dripping wet and most of the others are 2 or 3 years older and a lot bigger than me so my hand goes up for football along with a couple of other stick insects while the rest vote for rugby. Fuckin brutal game it should be banned.

I ended up in the scrum opposite Scouse who literally batters the daylights out of me, twisting my head and body in every direction possible and at times it felt he created new directions for a body to be manipulated. There was definitely an opportunity for scouse as a chiropractor in the legal world. Near the end of the game he charges towards me after battering through half my team like a cartoon bull with steam coming out of his ears and nose with the ball tucked under his arm. All my instincts are yelling at me to just move out of Scouse's way and let him score another try but I thought you've got to at least try to tackle him. I had a very small rugger knowledge and knew you sort of tackled by wrapping your arms round your opponent's waist and bringing them to the floor. So I launched myself arms outstretched to make what I was sure was about to be my first step on the ladder to rugby union legendary status. However, Scouse just sort of stopped his run and shoved his free palm full into my moosh and proceeded to squash me into the floor like an insignificant little insect then jogged over to complete his try.

Fucking brutal game, it should definitely be banned.

Oh well at least I tried I suppose.

In the showers Scouse informed me the move he had done to me was actually called a hands-off which was a fitting remark as Bronco Billy had appeared watching us all in the showers the filthy bastard.

As I was walking back to my cell I had just a towel wrapped round my waist and was absolutely freezing when out of nowhere Bronco appeared and stopped me putting his hand on my skinny little chest and said it don't look like they are feeding you well in here, would you like me to have a word so you get a bit more with each meal. Fuck me this proved the geezer was a wrong'un. I told him to fuck off or

I'll report ya you sick bastard and scooted round him and in to me cell.

Dee was back from his visit, looking stoned. He took one look at me and said who's give you a hiding, your face is battered? I explained it was Scouse at rugby which Dee found hilarious. I didn't tell him or anyone else what had happened with Bronco as I was embarrassed but I should have cos god knows what damage that bloke done over the years to many young vulnerable prisoners.

The whole of E wing were being taken to a big hall to watch a film and what was the movie selected for this group of impressionable young offenders? *McVicar*. A film based on the life of an armed robber who had escaped from Parkhurst maximum security nick and was captured after robbing a security van and subsequently moved to Durham prison - another maximum security prison - from which he somehow escaped yet again and was on the run for a couple of years. He apparently managed to get at Moors murderer Ian Brady and clouted him round the head with a chair.

As you can imagine we were all rooting for him throughout the film.

As we're all trooping back to E wing we're paused as they let a small amount of us through a locked door at a time. There is the smash of glass and a lot of shouting and pushing and shoving, the alarm goes off and some black lad falls to the floor with blood gushing out of his neck where he's cut his own throat.

The glass in the windows was all frosted and filled with wire, making them supposedly unbreakable. But somehow this lad had managed to put his arm through it and grabbed a chunk and slit his throat. Absolutely awful thing to witness and a terrible way to go for the young man with so much life ahead of him.

I hope he found his peace.

FOUR WALLS - PART TWO

During the coming 5 months we went back and forwards to court each time getting adjourned for a few weeks and each time the prosecutor would want us remanded in custody so we were in and out of the big holding cells at Lambeth. By now I had become one of the vultures who preyed on a new prisoner when they were thrown into the cell. You could literally smell the fear as they walked in and they were ripe for the taking.

Give us a burn have you got any gear blah blah blah - it just seemed like a never ending cycle. One time we're sitting in the holding cell when the door opens and a pretty large skinhead walks in. He's probably about 20 years old and out on the streets I'm sure would've looked intimidating but in here there are always people bigger and scarier and much more dangerous.

Now this Skin had a pair of large boots on with red laces. During the 70s and 80s this was a racist emblem. He couldn't have looked more out of place if he'd walked in wearing a white cloak and hat with KKK stamped on it. Straight away the black lads are on him. Why you wearing the red laces? Are you a Nazi? He suddenly understands he's well out of his league and totally outnumbered.

There's maybe 30 of us in the cell at the time and probably 20 were black lads and I'll be fucked if us few white lads are going to give him any back up. He looks to me and Dee for a bit of moral support but we let him know he's on his Jack Jones by passing a joint to Scooby. Anyway he's got them red laces in and I bet on the out with his mates he'd be steaming people of different colours.

Now it's payback.

I'd never been into any form of racist shit. I simply judged people on whether they were a wanker or not and if they were up for having an earner and getting stoned. If so, they were fine by me. Besides I'd always thought of myself as different from everyone so though I was white I always felt isolated. He spots some bloke from the outside world and says you know me from Wood Green you know I'm not racist. Bad luck for Mr Red Laces as the bloke ain't having none of it and says I've never seen you before in my life.

A few of the other lads start ringing the bell on the door and kicking and hammering the door shouting help, help I'm dying. No one comes. This was their way of knowing they can batter Mr Red Laces and no-one will come to his assistance. Kelly asks him if he wants twos up on his fag to which he says I don't smoke to which Kelly says bollocks it's cos you won't share a smoke with a black person.

Sometimes in certain situations you can feel the atmosphere like a layer of smoke engulfing the area and this was most definitely one of those occasions. The fag was square in Kelly's fist then bang full on smack in the face with the fist with the fag going straight in his eye. From then he took one of the worst, most savage hidings I have ever seen in my life. It must have gone on for a good 5 minutes, with him rolling round the cell like a football.

I am ashamed to say that me and Dee made it clear we were not witnesses to what was going on as at the end of the day it is self-preservation and we didn't know the bloke from Adam and owed him nothing. I'm sure if the boot was on the other foot he would have done the same, though I wouldn't have worn red laces in my boots.

Do you know when someone is hoovering the front room and when they get near you with the hoover you lift your legs so they can hoover underneath? Well that's what myself and Dee did each time Mr Red Laces rolled round. He was virtually unconscious when they were finished with him and when a screw finally opened the door to introduce a few new recruits they looked at the state of him lying there and you could see them thinking fuck me what've we just walked into?

The screw just said what's happened to him? Someone said it looked like he was having a fit and we tried helping but he was lashing out, we kept pressing the buzzer and calling for help but you totally blanked us.

Straight away this shifted the blame onto the jailers and that was that.

Mr red laces ended up in hospital and came into Ashford about a week later still covered in bruises but no one was charged for anything so he obviously said nothing. He did however ask to go into solitary confinement and the only other time I saw him was walking down the corridor accompanied by two screws, strangely minus his red laces.

After a while Stu and a few of the other more slightly elder inmates said I was just going to end up lost in the system like a lot of them. I had no idea what they meant. But it seems a fair few of them were looking at a fair few years when finally getting sentenced. Pleading not guilty, as pretty much everyone did, they could wear their own clothes (civvies) - as I was by now. You were also better off on remand cos once found guilty you would be shipped out to other nicks and whatever you'd already served would come off your sentence.

I was only up on a charge of trying to steal a couple of boxes of blank video tapes which, at worst, even though I had a small record by then, would get the proverbial slap on the wrist or probation. But as I'd already served just short of five months on remand, I would basically walk free if I just changed my plea to guilty.

By then I knew quite a few good people and though I was absolutely nowhere in the main pecking order I was liked, which is a big plus. My response to Stu was why the fuck would I plead guilty when realistically I only picked the boxes up and then got a good hiding off the manager and a few Old Bill, so in my mind I hadn't really committed an offense.

The way to look at it fella, Stu said, is you can sit in here stewing for another six months and then walk or contact your brief and tell him you're going to change your plea to guilty, and get seen in a couple of weeks and walk. At the end of the day I was told, you must have done dozens of things that you've got away with so just put your hands up to this one and take it on the chin.

Dee by then was due up pretty soon for sentencing on another charge and was definitely getting bird for that. The thought of being without him made me think, bollocks they're right, let's get out of here. So I got in touch with my brief who arranged for a hearing in seven days' time.

Due to changing my plea I was lobbed into A wing which was for people going back to court imminently. So it was back to see Mr T on reception who by now I was on talking terms with but still wary of. This time he blessed me with pants that actually fit. I was then put in a cell with a bloke my age who told me he was in for street robbery. He was referred to by each and every one as Mouse due to his darting, shifty-looking, rodent eyes.

I must admit I got on very well with Mouse, and on A wing this was a big plus being as you're banged up twenty-three hours a day. If you've ever had to spend a day shut in one room with nothing but a book and what is to all intents and purposes a stranger, it takes boredom to another level. You are left to just let your mind wander and there is nothing current to talk about as you've not seen nor spoken to anyone else for hours on end.

After a few days I was wandering round the yard when Dee shouted out from above Joe, that fucker Mouse is in for rape! No he ain't mate he's in for a street robbery he's a decent fella. No he ain't, trust me, mate, so and so has a copy of his file. Later while Mouse was out doing half hour exercise a screw opens the door with a prisoner who has a trolley full of books. Dee said you'll love this one and he gave me a copy of *Wuthering Heights* and the door was slammed shut.

Fuckin hell I like reading but reading about Heathcliff and all that wasn't really my cup of tea. As I open the book to leaf through it a folded paper falls out. As I open it, it has Mouse's real name along with his charge sheet. There it is in black and white: rape. The filthy rodent-looking little shit. And I've shared a room with the little tramp and I'm thinking I'm going to have to do something cos he's proper fed me a load of bollocks.

During lock up at night you had a pisspot for the obvious, then if you needed to take a dump and a half decent screw was on, you would ring your buzzer and eventually the screw would appear and you'd beg I need a shit guv, and if he was half alright he'd unlock the door and take you to the bog. Nowadays most cells have a toilet but then it was just a row of cubicles in which the door was only quarter the size of a full door so while sitting there doing your business you were visible to the screw from the chest up and the knees down.

Having a shit is a private almost ceremonious job, but should most definitely be a solitary occasion. But even the decent screws would keep tutting and looking at you as you're trying to shit out the shit the nick's been feeding you, all the while looking at their watch. The embarrassment of wiping your arse in front of someone else is also a very strange experience indeed.

If there were no decent screws on you would have to compromise. This would entail shitting in front of another human being, this time your cellmate. This is even worse than a screw gaping at you while doing what comes natural as you are in a tiny space together and there's no other way to put it other than its demeaning and fucking stinks. So you would gather some newspaper, crouch as far as possible away from your cell mate and do the business in the newspaper, wipe your arse on a piece of tissue if you're fortunate to have any, if not you scrape a piece of newspaper across the old butty hole. I'm sure if you bent over and looked in a mirror you'd be able to read the headlines on your arse. You'd then fold everything into a parcel as tightly as possible. The next job was getting rid of the parcel as swiftly as possible as the cell is your whole living area. You would push your head through the middle window and shout out shit bomb at the top of your voice so that anyone who was hanging out of their window talking or smoking would have time to duck for cover before the ensuing shit explosion. You would then launch your shit bomb into the yard below. This is where I should have put two and two together as I'd previously seen Mouse out there picking up the shit parcels mid-mornings - a job always given to those in for the more filthy and downright disgusting crimes.

Now I've said I'm not really a fighter but having spent a number of days with Mouse I had to do something or people would doubt me. If I'm being honest I really wanted to clump the little vermin anyway. So when he came back to the cell from exercise I waited till he was sat on his bunk and stood up and pissed in me pisspot and then full pelt clouted him round the head with it so forcefully it broke.

The horrible little shit faced rat just screamed like a little baby. The door opened and I was dragged out and thrown in a cell on me own. I felt fully justified in what I'd done and to this day I still do. I never even got to go in front of the governor for the offence and the following week I was up in court pleading guilty to trying to steal two boxes of blank vhs video tapes and walked out with two years' probation, telling myself I ain't going back there again.

It was time to get a job and crack on with my life in the real world. This lasted till I got home and went in my pub where I was treated like a returning war hero for fuck knows what reason.

Looking back, I was just a little nobody trying to be a somebody, which I wasn't in any shape or form.

A FEW RANDOM NICKNAMES AND A
BIT OF FOOTBALL

During the mid-80s to early 90s a little crowd of us would go over the football and followed our local team. We most definitely were not part of the main firm but did try our best to stick together. Especially when travelling to away games, we would check out the local shopping centres to see if they were clued up and if they weren't we soon gave them a short sharp lesson in security by emptying their shelves and goods which we'd either sell to other fans or wait till we got back home.

About 1986 myself and a mate known to us all as Lunchbox were seeing a couple of young ladies in an area in which our little area was at constant war with. To be honest it had been going on for generations and I have no idea what started it but there was a constant feud. If we went into their area or vice versa and was spotted it would kick off. Lunchbox was a good mate for many years and even now is referred to in that way rather than his real name - Colin.

A few years after Linford Christie was christened The Lunchbox, Colin tried turning it round that he was known by the name for the same reason, i.e. the size of his lunchbox. But it was most definitely not so. It was pure and simple down to the fact that wherever he went he always carried a lunchbox about with him. Even when he was going down the pub he would have his goodie box to snack on. He would have a cheese sandwich - always smothered in tomato sauce - a *Club* chocolate biscuit, a *Wagon Wheel* and either a *Kia ora* or *Um Bongo* carton of drink. I'd always try to beg a bit of his lunch and he'd point blank refuse saying bollocks you lot are always taking the piss out of me lunchbox and now you're hungry you all love me.

All sweet drinks and *Wagon Wheels* possibly backfired in later life as he is now type one diabetic and has to inject insulin into himself on a regular basis.

Anyway, back in the day Lunchbox was a handsome young bloke and we were seeing these two ladies who lived in a block of flats on an estate in our neighbouring foe's area. Now I say ladies as they were two sisters in their late twenties while we were both lustful late teens. Neither were the best of lookers but both were proper up for a good time and, as all young lads/young men of that age, we were led by our loins and weren't going to let an ugly moosh get in the way of a leg over.

Just in case they happen to be reading we'll call these two sisters Debbie and Louise. Debbie was the older by about 18 months and had a fella but he worked nights which is when we would pop round there for a few hours' fun. All we really had to do was take round a scores worth of Billy Whizz - which they both loved - and they were game for anything.

One-night, Lunchbox and I were cutting through the estate after a night's debauchery when we were spotted by a dozen or so of the locals. Words were exchanged from a distance but we were totally outnumbered. Lunchbox wanted to stand I told him bollocks to that and we eventually get chased off the estate and into the local shopping centre.

Maybe due to our sexual exertions we were both royally shagged and Lunchbox was grabbed and though he was game as he always was, he went down. I had to go back and try to back him up so I'm swinging windmill after windmill, of which I did manage to land a few wild haymakers, though I ended up on the floor getting kicks to the head and body. I was then picked up and unceremoniously launched through the window of the local Dixons electrical shop landing among shattered glass and some half decent electrical goods.

The little firm ran off, leaving Lunchbox flat out on the pavement and me in the window. Never one to miss a freebie I spotted a Sony hi fi that was sitting there literally calling me to not leave it all alone in that messy glass-strewn window. Always one to assist I grab the hi fi, minus the speakers, before scooping Lunchbox up - who was proper battered - and off we scuttled back to the streets we knew and felt safe on.

It was the next morning in the bath I saw how badly cut I was after my little window dive with slices down my side, both legs and a big shiv near my left ear. Now as I said we would go over the football with our little crowd and got to know a few other little mobs that would congregate near us. If we ever bumped into each other it would still kick off even though we all supported the same team.

Probably about a year or so after the window incident we were plotted up about 9pm on a Friday night in the local Chinese - which had a cab office next door - deciding where to go for the night. Half a dozen young fellas from our area come sprinting out of the nearby train station in a bit of a mess having been ambushed and chinned by a little mob in an area a few stops further down the train line. So we all scoot round the back of the Chinese where we have a stash of tools, half snooker cues, little bats etc. and straight in the cab office and within minutes were all in half a dozen mini cabs to gain some revenge for our wounded comrades.

We're driving round looking for em when the cab in front stops so we all follow suit and jump out. Hundred yards down the road is a little mob to which we're informed that's the slags. As far as they're concerned, it's fight or flight time. Well they decided on the flight mode as to be honest there were a fair few dangerous fuckers with us that night who would go on to do some serious bird for some quite dreadful attacks on others. Now I don't care who you are but if 30 odd people are charging towards you waving cues looking like they mean business it's a very basic human instinct to just turn and run.

So we're charging down the streets tooled up and we drift down different back roads till there's about 10 of us and within reach is one of their stragglers. Fella in front of me sweeps his legs and he goes down like the proverbial sack of spuds and curls up into a ball waiting for the inevitable onslaught that is surely about to come.

Just as he's lying there in that split second I see his face and recognise him from over the football. This changed everything. I'd stood with him over the football cheering on the boys and even shared a joint with him a couple of times on the concourse. So I just dive on top of him shouting no, no leave him alone I know him fuck off. The others look on in shock before bolting after the others, leaving us two.

Fucking hell mate nice one I owe you big time, he says. Too fuckin right you were about to get a right pasting there. I say quick fuck off cos if they don't catch anyone they'll be back looking for blood and I won't be able to stop them again. We shake hands, he bolts off and I catch up with a few of the others who had by then smashed up a few and were now looking to get out of the area.

To the station we went, victorious and happy as Larry (whoever he is), that we had got a bit of revenge and go back to the Chinese for a feast. Back then a feast was Chinese chips smothered in curry sauce washed down with vodka, a few joints and a line of speed.

Not long after this a fair little mob of us had met up early to go to an away London derby. We get off the train early and wander about down the King's Road looking for an earner. Being a football day it comes on top with a firm of the other mob's fellas and we end up scattered all over the gaff, till I'm left with a mate who's a year or so older than me and an absolute lunatic. Fearless John P was game as anyone and could also back it up with his fists. I did feel a bit safer having him by my side as we were wandering about on turf where we weren't welcome and it seemed every man and his dog wanted to give us a good hiding.

We make it safely into the away end which back then was a huge open stand with no roof and a few different sections. These were the days before mobile phones, so it was a matter of searching for our pals but it was rammed with literally thousands and in the end we just give up. Just before the game is about to kick off I glance to the side and I spot the fuckers who'd thrown me through Dixons window and they're about fifteen handed. I think fuck me you've got to be kidding, here we go at least there ain't no windows for em to launch me at. I say to John P. John it's going to go off mate, he says why what's the matter, I say that little firm there are the ones we always kick off with they're the ones who lobbed me at the window. John calm as you like just says no worries mate, I'm sorted.

Now as I say John is someone not to fuck with so I think ahh he's got a plan even though we're well outnumbered. He puts his hand in his jeans back pocket and proceeds to pull out that day's copy of the sun newspaper? A fuckin paper, John, what you going to fuckin do hypnotise em with Samantha Foxes boobs then read em their horoscopes by mystic Meg? No mate, he says, I'll batter em.

This is when I fully understand John is mad as a March hare and we are in deep shit - well I am, anyway. John folds his paper meticulously about five times and donks me on the head with it, feel that son, he says and fuck me it hurts but it ain't going to do this little firm. Me Chelsea brick John informs me, a lethal little tool that's why I always buy a paper. Meanwhile I'm looking round planning how we're going to get out of this one.

As I'm conspiring my escape who do I see but my man who I'd saved from a battering a few months prior purely cos I'd stood near him and shared a joint with him a couple of times. He was directly in front of John and I had about ten people separating us. He was with a proper decent looking crew and all I hoped was they didn't turn on me as well due to the fact a few of them had more than likely got caught that night I helped him out. Anyhow, in for a penny and all that. I shove past those in front of me till I'm face to face with the fella who I was hoping would remember me. I fall into him, pushing him into his pals. He turns round ready to rare up then clocks who I was. I just hope he don't think fuck you, your mates battered mine and then I'll end up with a couple of mobs on me case. Straight away he gives me a big bear hug and goes this is the fella I was telling you about who saved me that night. I seriously owe him. I say thank fuck for that cos it's payback time. Why what's the matter mate? I point to the left and say me and me mate are going to get served up by that little mob.

Him and his mates take one look at em and he says no you ain't, and they steam straight into the other mob. I look round and John's leaving the day's newsprint firmly embedded on a few of our foes and I get a few tasty boots at the wankers who lobbed me through the window myself. What goes around comes around as the saying goes and this occasion proved that big time. Strangely I'm now good pals with the main instigator of the window throwing mob and I would trust him with my life.

But that's another story.

JEWISH JACK

Many characters have come and gone during my fifty plus years, some good some bad and some plain rotten to the core. Jewish Jack at one point or other probably ticked all three boxes. He was known by everyone as Jewish Jack. Even his own mum referred to him as JJ.

Jack was about ten years older than myself. Our paths first crossed when we were out garden hopping - an innocent childhood pastime of running through as many gardens as possible without getting caught. Anyway this one time we were charging through these gardens at full pelt and this fella comes steaming out of the house in hot pursuit. For once my Sebastian Coe impression wasn't quite good enough and I was collared by Steve Ovett aka Jewish Jack. He gave me a proper good hiding, punching me and kicking me. I knew this was part and parcel of basically being a little shit, so I wiped the blood from me hooter and just had to accept it.

The above reminds me of a couple of other little digs I had as a youngster, the first being out garden hopping with one of my best friends I ever had - Gavin Dukes /known by all as The Duke. We were literally hurdling fences and gates laughing as only young kids do, when this fella who happened to be walking along the road took umbrage to our hopping technique and grabbed me and proceeded to beat the granny out of me with his briefcase. He was taking great delight in clouting me round the head with it, all the while my mate The Duke is hundred yards up the road in absolute hysterics. He never failed to remind me of the briefcase incident as we got older and we would always crack up over it.

Sadly, The Duke took his own life at the age of fifty.

There is much more involving this lovable, but very much misjudged and obviously troubled, character in a bit.

Another incident where I took a hiding as a youngster was a proper few digs off a grown man when I was about thirteen. What happened was we bumped into a little firm from another school one night but were completely outnumbered and took a few blows and I ended up with a fat lip, which for me is a common event as I have a terrible Dracula fang and if I get clumped it's an instant fat lip.

Anyway, one of these who jumped us had the misfortune to see me a few weeks later when I was poodling along on a push bike. His name was Kyle. Now, being by then quite light-fingered I knew only too well the benefits of having a chain to lock my stolen bike up to stop like-minded shits from having it away. I tucked the bike against a gate round the corner waiting for Kyle to appear. As he turned the corner bosh, full pelt round his nut goes the shiny thick bike chain. His mate took one look and decided that it wasn't the day to be a hero and was off like the wind. I was fully expecting that to be the end of the matter but unbeknown to me Kyle was rushed to hospital and had to have a large amount of stitches in his wounded barnet. Just my luck, turns out his old man is a bit of an old school face and is going to make sure he gets the fucker who did this to his boy.

A few days later about a dozen of us are in a mate's back garden sniffing glue when the side gate burst open and in strides Kyle's younger brother, accompanied by a very beefy looking old man both obviously out for revenge. The old geezer had muscles on his muscles and I just thought oh fuckin shit I'm going to get filled in big time here. He made us all stand against the fence and one at a time asked our names and said he was looking for Joseph Spencer.

Now I may have been a horrible little bastard at times but I really weren't thick and wasn't about to tell him my real name. He gets to me and says what's your fuckin name? Now being lads who tended to get into trouble of some kind every day we all had names and addresses that we knew off by heart of the well behaved local kids, so if old bill especially pulled us then checked the name we were going to be okay. As I got older the old bill knew me by sight and name instantly. I give the old man my best innocent look and look him straight in the eye and say Mark Jolly. He moves on and everyone gives him their names and he says tell Joseph when I see him I'm going to kick shit out of him for what he done to my Kyle.

Me being me I couldn't resist a little mumble of yeah whatever. He turns and says you say something dickhead? No mate, sorry. Just as he's about to fuck off, Kyle's brother says to his dad that one who said he's Mark Jolly is Joseph dad. Bollocks. I'd so nearly swerved it but no way was I going to even attempt to go toe to toe with a bloke who looked like he'd give the Incredible Hulk a run for his money in the muscle department, I just went full tilt for the fence. This was a typical six feet council fence with slats going down and a beam in the middle.

My intention was to land on the middle beam with my feet, both hands grab the top and scramble over into the street and to safety. Unfortunately, I missed the middle beam, smashed into the fence and crumbled and landed at the old man's feet. He picked me up by my head and gave me a full on man's punch in the moosh. Have that! The old Dracula tooth went straight through me lip and blood instantly gushed out.

If I thought that'd be the end I was mistaken, he punched me in the head a couple more times, and just for good measure Kyle's brother joins in the fun booting me in the nuts on behalf of his sibling. Not one of the fuckers in the garden thought to step in and help but if I'm being honest I don't blame them. We were kids and this was a man. Where d, ya live you little bastard, he shouts. I think thank fuck my mum will rescue me so I tell him. He doesn't let go of me till we get to my front door and my mum steams out what you doing get your hands off him.

I'm calling the police, Mum screams as by then I was covered in claret. He tells Mum all about the chain and Mum recites the line she's said for years and probably says in her sleep: Not my little Joseph. She would never believe anything bad about me. No matter what I'd done it was always someone else's fault. I had to admit to her this time it was me as I didn't want the old bill called.

Because:
1) it went against everything I had as far as morals go with not grassing

and

2) I would've got nicked for the little incident regards the chain.

Kyles old man ended up coming in and sitting down with my mum and step dad and became friends with them both, going down the working man's club with them for drinks and nights out. Many years later Mr Muscles would buy his weed from me and the incident of the chain and the good hiding he give me was never mentioned by either one of us.

Many moons and years on I now fully understand his reaction and would do exactly as he did to anyone who hurt one of my children or, God forbid, my grandchild. I've grown as a person since and have full respect for anyone who defends their family. If you live a certain way you cannot expect to walk away without any repercussions and I fully got what I deserved.

When I was about twenty this fella comes in the pub where I was selling puff/dope, acid plus a few other pills for good measure. Straight away I recognise its Jewish Jack. He says can I get ounce of draw mate. I've never been one to let holding a grudge get in the way of earning a pound note so duly said yeah mate and sorted him out and from there we became close. I never once brought up him chinning when he caught me garden hopping.

After a couple of years, me and Jack were partners of sorts and were selling dope as quick as we could get our hands on it. At one point the local we used - The Partridge - had about ten different people selling and serving up the community. It got to the stage it was so busy we would take it in turns to sell, unless we had our regulars who we would often give on tic. At some point me and Jewish Jack ended up falling out over something or other and went our separate ways but not before I'd chored a kilo of gear off him, which back then came in at about two grand, so wasn't to be sniffed at.

After a time, Jack went downhill fast. He tried smack and loved it and became addicted to it and went from having cash coming out of his ears to no matter how much he had it went straight in his veins with a needle full of the Devil's shit. Next thing I hear Jack's going about telling everyone he's got a shotgun and that little wanker Joseph - owes him a couple of grand plus interest and he fully intends to shove it up me arse. Jack would appear outside one of the local pubs I'd be in and I'd get a warning from a barmaid saying you'd better disappear, Joe, Jewish Jack's outside. I'd do a quick disappearing act through beer gardens and clambering out of toilet windows but in truth never really thought he had a shooter let alone would shoot me. However, I should have known that a smack head without gear is a highly dangerous individual, is absolutely fearless and will do anything to get their next fix. Add to the fact I owed him a large chunk of wedge he was, at the very least, genuinely going to let me know he weren't to be fucked with.

About four or five months of us going our different ways I hadn't heard anything about him in a while, I assumed he'd moved out of the area or was perhaps banged up, I assumed. Lesson to be learned here: never let your guard down with someone you've knocked especially if they've got a habit to feed.

There was an amusement arcade which we regularly robbed, and the owner Malcolm liked me for some reason even though he caught me regularly ripping open the back of the fruit machines in his shop with a toffee hammer trying to thieve the coins.

At various times we would wait till Malcolm was out the back, clamber behind the machines and jemmy one open and empty all the coins. Sad thing was he was actually a decent bloke who would let us loiter in his shop for whatever reason. But back then if anyone was nice to me it was a sign of weakness and they were there to be taken advantage of.

Looking back now as a completely different individual I cringe thinking what an absolute vile little wanker I was, and if I could bump into my old self now I would smash the fuck out of myself. But you live and learn and sadly I was horrid. I suppose I can blame drugs, or the fact I was spoilt or a million different excuses but I can blame no-one but myself and to every person I've hurt I truly hope they can forgive me, but if you can't I fully understand.

My way of looking at things now is like a mirror. When I look in the mirror now I know hundred percent that the person looking back at me is a decent person with a heart as big as the Thames who will help anyone at all. To look past myself in the mirror is looking backwards and all I try to do now is look forward and be kind. At one point I stole the coins from one of Malcolm's machines while he was out the back making me a cup of tea. (Honestly how low can you get?) I ran out of the shop and he charges out and grabs me so my only means of escape was to nut him - which I did right across the bridge of his hooter - and off I flew.

Believe it or not I still had the front to go back in his shop a couple of days later playing his fruit machines with the money I'd got from the back of one of em a couple of days prior. Turns out Malcolm has a big fuck off nephew called Mehmet the Turk. He fronts me out for nutting his uncle but for whatever reason I win him over and he takes to me and shakes my hand. Rather than learning how close I'd come I carried on smashing the backs off Malcom's machines and nicking the coins.

A couple of years on I'm visiting a mate in The Ville. I'm walking towards the place and Mehmet's bird - who is a proper stunner - calls out oi Joseph what you doing down here? A mate sent me a VO so I'm just popping in to see him. I ask where she's going, she tells me Mehmet chopped up a couple of fellas with an axe and is on remand. It turned out Mehmet was a total fuckin loon with an axe and I proper got away with a liberty by nutting his uncle.

I digress, back to Jewish Jack. One day I come bowling out of the amusement arcade and head to the pub but decide to pop down the alley by the train line for a piss first. Just as I'm unzipping me flies I hear a deafening noise and my leg goes from under me. I just sort of tumble to the floor with my trousers round me ankles. Turns out it's Jewish Jack and he actually does have a gun like he said and the bastard's fired at me and hit my shin. I've had a few clumps in my time but this pain is another level. I'm told I passed out and came round in hospital with Old Bill waiting to ask me questions to which I said absolutely jack shit about Jewish Jack. I didn't actually see Jack so it could have been anyone who I had upset but deep down I know was Jack. Although I have a savage scar on my shin from that shot, luckily it only grazed me as Jack was more than likely stoned at the time so thank God for small mercies.

Or in this case small sharp needles.

It just so happens not only did he have a shooter but Jack was charging about like Jesse James robbing betting shops with it. He copped a twelve stretch and wrote me asking if I'd visit him. I decide to go and see what he has to say and he tells me point blank he fired at me but said thanks for not saying anything to the Old Bill. We agree the money I knocked him for was done and dusted and I had a little war wound to remind me not to rip off a junkie.

Jack ended up going into the drug rehabilitation wing where they get tested regularly and if they fail they're back in the system, whereas if you stay clean you get time off your sentence. I think he went on to serve about seven years and we stayed in touch the whole time.

Sadly, Jack had a bad ending a few years later but before I tell you about that, more about my troubled, misunderstood friend, The Duke.

The Duke THE GREAT CONVINCER

The Duke was my first proper friend, not just a mate - a true friend. We met in the infants and maybe cos we were both a bit odd we just clicked from day one. We would stay at each other's houses while our parents went out together and would even go on holiday together.

Even though The Duke would go on to be one of the toughest men I ever encountered both physically and mentally he started out being bullied and beaten at school. Each day the school hard nuts (or so we all believed that's what they were) would wait at the gates and use The Duke as a punch bag.

As I've said many times, I was not a particularly brave lad. If I'm being honest I was a coward and sadly I never stepped in to help when help was needed. How I did help was the fact the bullies knew me and The Duke were friends, though back then he was simply known by them as Gavin the punch bag. At home time, The Duke would wait in the school bogs and I would walk out of one gate and the bullies would surround me asking where's your boyfriend we've got something for him. While they were haggling me The Duke would slip out the other gate.

True friends stand by you through thick and thin and The Duke more than repaid my meagre efforts to get him out of his daily beatings at school as he got older and became The Duke. I'm not sure of when precisely, but as he hit senior school he decided he was going to stand up for himself and hit back. From that moment I think he realised he could not only defend himself but he could be one seriously hard bastard if the need arose.

Years on we're in a pub and one of the above mentioned bullies comes up and says hello and asks ain't it that little prick Gavin? I just say you might want to do yourself a favour and disappear sharpish cos he really ain't that little boy you used to chin at the school gates.

The Duke comes walking up and just holds his hand out and shakes his old aggressor's hand while looking him in the eye and letting him know he made his early life a misery and he was going to give his hand a proper squeeze. The bully sizes up The Duke - who by now is more than twice his size - and chooses the wisest course of action which is to apologise profusely and offer to buy him a drink. In fairness, The Duke could by then have done him some serious damage but he let it go, which shows the measure of the man in my eyes.

Me and The Duke would get up to all sorts of mischief. I remember us being very young lads about ten years old and we decided we liked the look of all the Action Men and all the paraphernalia that went with them - tanks, boats, sand bags, the lot - in the local Debenhams. We stuffed everything we could in the tank and waltzed down the escalators, and out of the door to be grabbed by a couple of store detectives. We were taken to a little room while they decided what to do with us.

Back then kids weren't treated so leniently as now and the police were called even though we were under age. We were taken home and my mum's mantra of not my little Joseph was once again uttered from the great lady's mouth. I convinced her it was all a mistake and we were just playing with the Action Men and didn't realise we had walked out of the store without knowing what we were doing. She was convinced of my good virtue and honesty and my punishment from Mum was a visit to the local Wimpy bar for a Brown Derby (ice-cream and a warm doughnut).

Those reading this have my full blessing to call me a spoilt manipulative little shit. And you would be totally correct. Another occasion myself and The Duke were offered money to smash up a car. It was an odd situation where about four or five fellas chipped in and purchased a Datsun sunny motor and shared it. One of the group accused the other few of knocking him for his share of the car and would never let him use it. Let's call him little Rob. Little Rob asks The Duke do you want to earn a bullseye (fifty pounds)? All you've got to do is cane all the windows on the Datsun. The Duke comes up to me in The Partridge and says if you want to earn a pony (Twenty-five pounds). All you got to do, he says, is wait till it's dark and we`re going to smash little Rob's Datsun for him. In for a penny in for a pony, count me in mate. We have a few bevvies in the pub then head off to do the deed.

Back then I regularly carried a little toffee hammer with me which I concealed down my sleeve. This was my tool of the trade for my pickings from the fruit machines and who knew when it would be handy as protection. The Duke chose a bar that he literally dragged, pulled and heaved out from someone's front evergreens. All the way there he kept saying right I'll do the front windscreen and two front headlights and you do the same at the back but wait till I say go so we can start and finish at the same time then have it on our toes and collect our money.

We're standing outside the house. The curtains are drawn but the lights are on. No-one about and we got our chosen ends of the Datsun. The Duke whispers to me wait till I count to three.

As I'm pausing in preparation, The Duke lets fly with his bar, smashing straight through the windscreen and getting a head start on me in the Datsun smash-up challenge. I smack the toffee hammer into the back window and go to pull it out and the house door bursts open and me and The Duke are off like the wind. Unfortunately, I was minus my toffee hammer which was still hanging out of the car window. It was dark by now and we easily lost whoever it was pursuing us and went round too little Robs to collect our bounty.

The next morning I'm strolling down a road about a mile or so away from where we'd smashed the Datsun and notice a lot of Old Bill cars and I see a Ford Granada which belongs to the dad of one of the other Datsun owner's, and lo and behold, my toffee hammer's embedded in the windscreen. What the fuck, how has that ended up there? I see this as an opportunity to get it back and go to grab it.

Don't touch that please young man we want that for fingerprints says a female copper. Oh sorry it's my mate's old man's motor and I was just going to take it out was my instant reply. I say shit I've touched it so my prints are going to be on it. I'm really sorry. Result. I've got away with that one.

Or so I think.

The following Sunday I'm having a lovely lay in when the early morning peace is broken by thumping on the door and voices shouting up oi Spencer you little shit Rob paid you to smash our car up. Oh fuck how am I going to wriggle out of this one? Mum, as she always has done, opens the door all seven stone of her and confronts em all. Not my little Joseph you must be mistaken he wouldn't do something like that.

They ease back from the door and shout up we heard it was you and The Duke was paid to smash it up. Come round to Chaz's old man house cos we thought it was Chaz who smashed the Datsun so we left the hammer in his old man's motor. Fuckin hell it's like an Agatha Christie novel - The case of the Reappearing Toffee Hammer.

As soon as they go I yet again convince Mum it's a complete misunderstanding and I'm going to go and get The Duke and we'll go round there and prove our innocence. I wake up The Duke who only lives five minutes away and tell him they thought Chaz had smashed the Datsun for some reason and they took the hammer and implanted it in his old man's Granada to make a point. A load of nonsense that had got out of hand. Jesus we only earnt a pony each. The Duke says right let me do all the talking and I'm going to convince em it's all a mistake. So off we go knock on the door and there's about seven of em sitting there giving us daggers. Right you two we've been told little Rob paid you to smash our motor up. Somehow The Duke sweet talks em into believing we had nothing to do with the whole episode while I just stand there nodding and looking thick. We're made tea and even get offered custard creams placed on a plate and they all apologised for even doubting our integrity. We looked dutifully shocked that they would even think so badly of us two God-fearing citizens.

We walk out of that house and out of the gate knowing not to look at each other cos we're both on the brink of bursting into hysterical nervous laughter. As soon as we get round the corner we crack up. Fuckin hell I says to The Duke you were in full flow there mate you were so good I ended up believing we hadn't done it. Honestly he could really get you hooked in. He once persuaded me to saw the little legs off the bottom of my stereo stack system so that it would fit into a unit, rather than get a different unit.

Truly a great convincer was The Duke.

JEAN MICHEL JARRE - PART ONE

While most people were raving I was selling pills, acid and dope and going to rock concerts. Although I sold a large amount of illegal chemicals, there was a time I was selling what lads thought were LSD tabs but were in fact little pieces of Embassy fag packets.

Everyone had gone to a rave and I was just sitting in The Partridge with a couple of mates having a beer and smoke when half a dozen lads come in and ask if there's any acid about. We say come back in an hour and we'll see what we can do. Back then a load of us carried little Stanley knives about for chopping things etc. and one of my mates had a pack of twenty Embassy Number One. I carved his box up and created a dozen or so little squares and said they could easily pass as acid. If them bods come back, I'm going to punt em these at a fiver a pop. You'll never get away with that Joe mate. I say you never know unless you give it a bash.

Shortly after the lads return and I say yeah I've managed to get twelve acid tabs but only take one each tonight cos I've been told they're proper potent. Sixty quid was passed and they received their twelve unbeknown to them placebo acid / Embassy Number One fag packet bits. They sodded off and me mates said Joe you've got some serious front mate when they clock you've sold em shit they'll be back. But they were more than happy to help me spend the sixty notes that night.

The following weekend I'm sitting in The Partridge just me and a pal Richard all on our jacks when the door opens and here's my acid popping lads along with another few mates. I'm thinking bollocks here we go they're all going to steam me and Richard won't even back me up. Hello mate one of em says with a big smile I don't know if you remember me but I came in last week and bought twelve acid off you have you got any more they're pukka mate?

You couldn't make it up.

Yes, mate come back in half hour, how many you want? How many dya reckon you can get? Twenty or thirty. Yeah, as many as you can get, best acid we've ever popped.

They fucked off and soon as they were out of sight I ran round the off licence and bought forty Embassy Number Ones, back to the Partridge and carved up thirty acid/Embassy fag packet bits. Back they come eager as a dog on heat and I say, as you're buying bulk I'll do the lot for hundred and twenty. Off they go again wherever it was, they went tripping in their minds but in fact had chewed a tiny little piece of a fag box.

This went on for a good few months and it became a standing joke in the pub where everyone would say how many Embassy you sold this weekend Joe? I like to think in my own small way I helped these lads who were only a few years younger than me from ever having a bad trip or getting the horrors, but strangely they never once bubbled and just vanished after a time. Just say no to drugs, kids.

Jean Michel Jarre was a musician who created an album titled *Oxygene* which he performed in Paris to over a million spectators. No lyrics, just music, standing there doing a mental light show with a pair of white gloves on. I'm sure half of Paris would've been on acid that night and now he was coming to perform in London in the docklands and would surely be a Godsend for people looking to buy acid. Me being me I invested for the occasion in as many carefully carved Embassy Number Ones as possible, with just a little coloured motif on each one.

People must have thought I'd lost the plot walking round picking up empty fag packets and asking the bloke behind the bar to save them for me. For whatever reason, though the bar keepers name was Paul, he was referred to by us all as crab stick bollocks and even responded to it. Who knows how the fuck that name came about but it sounds painful.

Weeks of preparation went into the Jean Michel Jarre show on my behalf and the way I saw it was loads of gullible people wanting to pop an acid while buzzing to the music and light show and there was going to be upwards of a hundred thousand in attendance so the chance of me getting rumbled on my little scam was remote. As always though for me nothing was simple and in the weeks leading up to the event I had the misfortune to cross paths with the Fordham family.

The Fordham's

The Fordham's were a family of six brothers and a sister who had a very large input and output into most nefarious dealings in all corners of London and Kent as well as their domain in Essex. Raymond was the eldest - probably in his early forties when I encountered him in the late 80s - and was known as a very hard but fair bloke as long as you were honest with him, though he would go on to slap me round the face on more than one occasion.

Next up was Frank, an absolute savage of a human being who could put the fear of God into the devil himself. Then sister Veronica, known as Ronnie, who looked like a Rottweiler chewing a wasp and was known to fight like most men. After her there was Curly Fordham. While all the others were fair haired and light skinned Curly was very dark skinned and had a mop of jet black curly hair. I never knew nor asked Curly's actual name but there was a whispered rumour that he was the result of an affair that the Fordham's mother had while the old man was inside for a wage snatch. Curly seemed to have a constant chip on his shoulder, and was always going out of his way as if to prove he could be as nasty and vindictive as any of his family to play down the rumours he wasn't a Fordham.

Then came the twins David and Mason, always together and almost literally joined at the hip. Even when both got married they would always be out together with their respective other halves. Bringing up the rear and last but not least of the Fordham clan was Greg, whom every man and his dog suspected was gay, though no-one would ever say it to his face.

About a fortnight before the Jean Michel jarred show I'm sitting in The Red Lion pub where I knew most people when the door opens and in swaggers Raymond, Frank and Veronica Fordham along with a couple of huge security type blokes and finally a man mountain I'd had the misfortune to have had a little run in with by the name of Northern Jerry.

About a year or so before I tried to enter a club and had a considerable amount of contraband confiscated by the doorman - Northern Jerry. I'd been drinking vodka that night and was also trying to impress a couple of girls giving it the big I am when in truth I was just a little nobody in the grand scheme of things. I fronted Jerry and told him I knew his boss Raymond blah blah blah and I was going to make sure he fuckin learns who he's messing with, though in truth at that moment in time Raymond had no idea who I was.

Have that you mouthy little no mark Northern Jerry said and floors me with one punch and my attempts to impress went slightly wonky.

It's taken me years but I now understand its sometimes best to keep your mouth tightly sealed cos you really don't know who is who. Northern Jerry had the audacity to take me into the VIP section of the club with blood dripping down my lip from my Dracula fang, embarrassment following me along like a bad smell. He then chucked me over the roped off area of the VIP section and said sorry Mr Fordham, but this one here says he's your friend and you're supposed to tell me about the error of my ways.

A couple of ladies picked me up and I stood there like a clown at a funeral completely out of place. I told them he's lucky he caught me unawares or I'd have proper filled him in. Raymond and his entourage look at each other and burst out laughing. Cheeky fucker says Raymond, you're lucky you're still awake, after Jerrys give you a clump its normally lights out. Get him a drink Jerry says Raymond. The look on Jerrys face told me he wishes he'd jumped on me head instead of bringing me inside. Vodka and lemonade with extra ice for my lip please Jerry mate I say through my blood spattered teeth in my best brummie accent, knowing full well he was from Middlesboro but deliberately trying to wind him up.

Raymond asks what happened and I tell him I had a few pills and acid tabs and speed and Northern Jerry had taken it all off me. It was explained in no uncertain terms that anyone selling in here did so on behalf of the Fordham's or not at all. I spent half hour in Raymond's company and it was like sitting with royalty. Proper naughty looking people would come up and shake his hand and give him little hugs like something out of *The Godfather*. He then said to me right it's time for you to leave Mr Spencer and escorted me to the front door where he told Northern Jerry to return everything he'd taken off me earlier.

I should have just taken my wares along with my smashed face and fucked off but couldn't resist a wink at Northern Jerry and telling him you were lucky you done me with a sucker punch. He just glared and told me to piss off.

Anyhow I'm in The Red Lion and in comes Raymond and his little crew, walking in like they own the gaff. For all I know they very well could've done. They sit down and none of them go to the bar but the gaffer comes out and greets Raymond like a king taking all their orders and refusing payment.

There was a big crowd of us younger lot, late teens to late twenties plus an elder crowd in the other corner. Normally we were all raucous and full of it and if a little group of strangers walked in they would know instantly it was a local's gaff.

But soon as Raymond and his little group walked in everyone's head went down and eye contact was avoided. After quite possibly The Red Lion's quietest most peaceful half hour ever one of Raymond's chap's bowls over and says which one sells a bit of puff. I thought I'm saying nothing and not getting involved here but straight away old Nelly an old girl points to me and says Joseph sells the best spliff on the market.

Thanks Nelly, nice one.

Now Nelly was in her late 80s but was one seriously clued up old girl. A proper old Cockney girl she had lived through both wars and outlived most of her family and most of her children and all us in The Red Lion had become like her new family. She was always on our earhole for a brandy or a Guinness and would give us a song for a drink. *The Green Green Grass of Home* by Tom Jones, *Oh Danny Boy*, *Maybe it's Because I'm a Londoner*, and loads of others - her repertoire was large and whether you wanted to hear or not she'd come in and say get us a brandy Joey boy and I'll sing you a song. She was a grand old girl and we would all look after her and make sure she had fish and chips or pie and mash and a few of us would always make sure she got safely home to her house. She got many of us to try her snuff. Absolutely awful stuff it was but it felt bad to refuse such an old duchess so we'd end up sniffing speed or coke and snuff all in one.

One time half a dozen of us had to carry her home as she was so drunk she couldn't walk, the landlord letting us carry her home in the chair she'd fell asleep in. While trying to put the key in her street door cars pull up, blue lights flashing, and a little gang of Old Bill come charging up the gateway wanting answers on what we're doing with this vulnerable old lady.

Nelly wakes up and gives them a proper old mouthful, you leave my boys alone they are little angels and have hearts of gold.

But they are known to be involved with drugs, madam, says the coppers.

Don't be so stupid they would never do no such thing. She said this even though she saw us buying and selling virtually each day in the pubs. As I say she was one very clued up old girl.

The old bill had to leave with their tails between their legs.

Raymond's man asks me if he can take an ounce for him to sample? Bollocks. I'm left with no choice but to pass over the oz. At that time, it was worth about £120 cut up or £85 a lump. Raymond's mob proceeds to roll a few joints and after ten minutes Northern Jerry stands up and says Joseph you've been knocked, and bangs his hand on the table in a knocking gesture. I can see he took great delight in embarrassing me in front of the whole boozer but what the fuck can I do other than my best fronting it out technique. The money for that oz. was owed to someone else so I had to at least make an effort to reclaim it and that way the fella who I owed it to would at least hear that I confronted Raymond and risked a good hiding in the process.

A mate says Joe you're fuckin mad mate just take it on the chin.

Bollocks to that.

I go to the table and say I'm really sorry but is anyone going to pay for that cos I owe the money out?

Jerry sees this as another chance to deck me properly this time but Raymond, thank the Lord, remembered me.

He cracks up and says this little fucker has some serious nerve and shouts get him a vodka and lemonade with ice. Take a seat young man. He tells Jerry to go and get me my drink and I say cheers Jer in a scouse accent and if looks could kill I'd have died on the spot. Raymond then tells me you should never at any cost just part with merchandise without payment unless you are prepared to go to war to get your cash. He says you son have got some serious spunk coming to my table especially knowing Jerry wants to measure you up for a coffin. Jerry comes back and gives me my drink with a glare. Jerry pay the lad his money.

Fuckin hell you couldn't make this shit up.

He offers me £75 and I have to inform him it's £85 and he begrudgingly throws another tenner at me. It's time for you to go Joseph but I feel perhaps you could do a bit of work on my behalf - a statement not a question. What would that entail Mr Fordham? I'll give you a thousand window pane acid tabs on credit for three quid each, but you do not and I repeat do not give any out to anyone without payment cos this is my money and if you fuck up Jerry here will be delighted. Thank you Ray I'd be well chuffed. He tells me his address and to pop round at midday the following day. Now off you go Joseph and one last thing, only my wife calls me Ray, never call me that again. Sorry Mr Fordham.

JEAN MICHEL JARRE - PART TWO

(AND TWO BOXES OF MATCHES)

I went and sat back at the table with my mates giving it the big'un. My arse had stayed intact and I now was going to be grafting on behalf of the Fordham's. I caned a few more vodkas then decided to get home and get me head down.

Next morning, I woke early and for the first time in ages wasn't sure how to dress for the occasion. I had a suit I wore for court and put that on as Raymond was always suited and booted but when I looked in the mirror it screamed you look like a right prick so I just threw a pair of 501s on and Fred Perry shirt, which is a brand and style I have always loved and still wear to this day. I had planned my journey and would need to get a couple of trains and a bus. I left my house with plenty of time to get there and was hoping to stop at a pub near to where Raymond lived for a bit of Dutch courage.

I had a spring in my step as I made my way to the Central Line for the first part of my journey imagining how my life was about to take off. I had grand visions of this being the beginnings of my climb up the Fordham empire and that one day I would have Northern Jerry crawling round at my behest. Half a dozen stops later and I have to jump on the District Line heading into unknown territory and I start getting a bit paranoid. I make it to within a couple of miles by then I have to jump on a bus to take me near to Ray's gaff. I decide to go in a betting shop first and do a line of speed to perk me up a bit. Big mistake. I start getting even more paranoid, walking these streets that are so unknown to me.

Waiting at the bus stop some big fella standing there gave me a dirty look and I suddenly get it into my head that I'm on my way to Raymond's to get proper filled in. Stranger things have happened. I think if he gets on my bus

I'm going back home while I'm still breathing. My bus pulls in. I have an old style bus pass that you scratch off the day and date that I've been using for months without getting sussed. I flash it at the driver and sit down thinking thank fuck they don't have clippies still out here in the sticks which is how I thought of the area. Gazing out the window everything seems to me to have an air of menace.

The old girls walking along with their shopping trolleys and head scarves I'm convinced are watching me knowing full well where I'm going and that I'm heading for a nasty end. I should never have done that fuckin line, I always thought I needed a line or a joint but with hindsight realise all they did was make me as paranoid as fuck. A bloke walking a Staffy glances at the bus as we we're sat at a set of lights and catches my eye and it's more than likely just an innocent nod of the head but in that moment I'm thinking Jesus the whole fuckin area is in on this elaborate plan to rid the world of me. So, me being me, I discreetly put a bit of wizz in the join between my thumb and finger and hoover it up like a pro.

That'll help, I think.

What a dopey knob. It just made things worse.

I know I've got a twenty-minute walk from when I get off to Ray's gaff so when I see my stop I jump off full of horrors and search out a pub, thinking if I neck a couple of vodkas that'll sort me out. I spot a lovely little pub and stroll in to see one man and his dog sitting in there. I go straight up the ramp and get a neat double vodka, wallop then order another and go and sit in the corner by the window to try and get me head in gear. The vodka's hit the spot and I'm back to the usual cheerful Jack the lad Joseph or Spence again. Hitting the street again I'm in much better spirits eyeing up the local rich girls, thinking soon I'll be working for Raymond and these birds will be all over me like a rash.

I really was a twat.

The houses round there were massive and all were gated. So I'm was strolling along admiring the houses when lo and behold I hear a car pull up with two uniformed Old Bill inside. They don't get out but ask what I'm up to as they haven't seen me round here before and everyone knows everyone and someone had reported a stranger in the manor. I tell em I'm just popping to see a mate, Mr Fordham. I think shit if they search me I'm fucked what with the speed and puff in me pockets but they just say it's the last house at the corner you have to buzz for someone to come to the gate to let you in and I hope you're not late cos Raymond hates tardiness. I thought no way even the Old Bill know I'm about to either get murdered or am picking something up from Raymond. But off they drive wishing me a nice day. I couldn't believe it. I keep going towards the corner, each house getting more grand than the one before with each step.

And then I'm greeted by the walls and gates of chez Fordham.

I stand there looking at the wall and the gate but for the life of me I can't find the fuckin buzzer. I'd left the pub at half eleven and had been walking for at least half hour so I know I'm now probably late to meet the great man.

I panic and decide in my vodka and whizz brain to jump over the wall. I put my hands on the top and heave myself up till I'm squatting on top of the wall admiring Raymond's palatial entrance when I realise my hand is stuck to the wall. Ahhh for fuck sake I was covered in black anti climb paint. Just like a thick tar it's all over me 501s and trainers as well as me hands.

Suddenly barking and snarling two Dobermans come steaming at me so I jump back down to the outer perimeter shitting myself and covered in tar. The gate bursts open and there's Northern Jerry with a grin the size of Blackwall Tunnel pointing to the buzzer that I'd missed. He calls me a dickhead and says you're late you prick. I enter the property with the two Doberman now trotting alongside Northern Jerry and me and he says if I was to tell Zeus to attack he'd rip you to shreds your horrible little vermin.

I tell him I really get the feeling you don't like me Jer are all Geordies so angry?

I ain`t a fuckin Geordie you little prick he says and I see he would love to set the dogs on me and would have great delight in assisting them.

Raymond appears at last from a sliding patio door, takes one look at me and says you look like a fuckin tramp why didn't you use the buzzer?

Sorry Mr Fordham I couldn't find it and didn't want to be late I blurted.

Well you are late and that's not a good start for any form of business, but I'm going to overlook it the once.

I was expecting to be shown round the house now that I felt I was part of the firm, or so I thought. Raymond soon put that notion to bed when he threw two Swan Vesta match boxes at me and said there's five hundred in each box but I've upped the price to four notes each cos you were late, now off you go. I'm thinking fuckin hell I'm going to have to punt these for at least seven quid each to get a little earner. Thank you Ray I say before my brain can stop the words. Immediately he grabs me and says Joseph what did I tell you my wife is the only person who calls me that and he slaps me full on round the face and tells me to piss off and make sure not to fuck up and that Jerry would find me in a few weeks for the money.

Jerry walks me to the gates with the two dogs by his side. I can feel my face burning where Raymond has slapped me and, to add insult to injury, Jerry says you can leave the same way you came - over the wall, dick head. Oh come on Jerry I plead with the face that has wrapped my mum round her little finger for years but to Jerry I'm just like a turd on the bottom of his shoe. That don't work with me he says, I am going to count to ten then set Zeus on ya.

He starts counting . . . one . . . two . . .

I know full well he isn't fuckin about and I scramble up the wall and stand on the top, now completely covered in the black anti climb paint, and just before jumping down into the street I turn and point to the floor where Zeus had just done a steaming shit and say in a Scottish accent better clean that up before Raymond steps in it, Jer.

And I'm on my way covered in shit with two match boxes with enough acid in them for a serious amount of people.

I pop into the pub, again the only life still present the same one man and his dog. I order a double vodka and lemonade and pop in the bog to check the acid. Now window panes are a very decent acid /lsd tab. The advantage of these is the fact that a normal acid is chewed and swallowed and can take anywhere from half hour to an hour before it starts to work. With a window pane you can place them direct on the eyeball and it's a pretty instant come up.

All looked present and correct so I think I'll try one to see what they're like. I place the window pane in my eyeball and I swear before I'm walking out of that pub a quarter of an hour later I'm tripping. The journey to Raymond's had been a paranoid extravaganza, but the journey home was spent laughing to myself. I befriended a strange bloke on the train instead of my usual lamppost and most likely left him wondering what the fuck had just occurred on his way home from work with some bloke with a twinkle in his eyes telling him all about how he had ended up covered in tar cos I'd fallen into a newly tarmacked road and how everything in life was just so beautiful man, even his tie I reliably informed him was just too beautiful and I insisted I had to buy it from him. He unfastened his tie at the next stop and said you can have it and jumped off just as the doors closed. I ran to the train doors. I'm guessing he was traumatised.

All the clothes I wore that day including my trainers had to be binned and the anti-climb paint stayed on my hands for weeks.

Over the next few days I managed to get rid of quite a few of the acid and fully intended on getting all of Raymond's money together before I started spending any of my profits. Besides I'd be able to sell them a tenner a go at the Jean Michel Jarre Docklands show soon. Bit by bit and vodka by vodka and popping acid and giving them out to mates I'd got rid of about 200 but had hardly any money left to show for it.

So come the day of the Jean Michel Jarre show I'm determined I'm going to stay sober and not touch anything cos once I start I can't seem to control myself. On the day of the show I stayed indoors all morning till I was ready to head to the Docklands. About lunchtime I left the house with a bit of money in my pocket and the two swan vesta match boxes full of acid.

As I'm walking towards the station just my fuckin luck from behind a bus stop there's two Old Bill who I know and they know me. Hello Joseph what you up to? They say just before you pass away your whole life flashes before you. Well in that split second every kind of thing went through my mind and my brain instantly kicks into overdrive. Everything rushes through my head at once. I'm thinking shit, shit, hippie Dean recently got five years behind the door for a similar amount of acid. Fuck I'll be all on me own in there and there's no way I'll be able to handle it. Poor little Joseph I thought, I ain't really bad oh shit, oh bollocks what am I gonna do? Nothing just on my way to the Docklands, I say. So you won't mind turning your pockets out then one asks. No, course not, I say trying to remain calm with my hand squeezing the two Swan Vesta boxes in the pocket of my jacket. What's that black stuff on your hand one of the Old Bill says noticing the anti-climb paint that I've been unable to completely remove. I tell him I fell in some tarmac.

The Old Bill go through my jacket and have just had me turn out my left trouser pocket while I keep one hand on the Swan Vesta boxes full of acid tabs in my right, the contents of which hold the key to me being locked up for at least half a decade. My brain screams at me to run. What's in there he says nodding to my right trouser pocket.

And at that moment, I bolted. Thank fuck this was before the Jewish Jack incident cos from that day on I've had a slight limp and nowhere near as swift on my toes.

JEAN MICHEL JARRE - PART THREE

I charge for The Partridge just round the corner, hit the door with me shoulder and launch the two match boxes of acid tabs into the pub and jump over the bar. In hot pursuit, the two Old Bill burst in a bit behind me and I'm swiftly dragged out of the pub with old Nelly yelling leave him alone he's a good lad is that joseph. Unfortunately, Nelly's pleas fall on deaf ears and I'm thrown against the outside wall of the pub for all the shoppers to gape at like a common criminal, and I'm thinking don't they know I work for the Fordham's?

Honestly, I was such a prick it makes me shudder.

The Old Bill make a call and a meat wagon turns up into which I'm unceremoniously lobbed in the back of. Just as the meat wagon's about to leave the pub door opens slightly and Lunchbox gives me a very quick thumb up and shuts the door. I am hoping he's giving me a thumbs up cos he's found the match boxes and then I can at least dig myself out of the mess of owing Raymond a few grand. I get to the station and am immediately strip searched, up the jacksie the lot, but they find nothing. Have a good fondle, did ya? What you run for then? Cos I like running, what you chase me for? Where did you say you was going? Jean Michel Jarre in Docklands I say with a smile. No you ain't we've got a bed for you for the night. Bastards.

And I'm lead to the cells.

I lay there that night once again pleading with all the gods and spirits to please, please get me out of this mess and I'll sort myself out. But yet again there is no flash of light or eureka moment and I'm just left to annoy the Old Bill. The copper on that night has got one eye and we all kept shouting oi one eye and throwing insults at him for our enjoyment. Is your Mrs a prossie, if not tell her I want me money back and stuff to that effect. What a bunch of nasty pricks we were.

I'm out the following morning with no charge but gutted that I never got to go to the show and earn some wedge. I get home and have a bath to scrub the smell of the Old Bill station from my skin and there's a knock at the door and straight away I think the worst - that it's going to be Northern Jerry to finally do his worst. But I look out the window and its Lunchbox.

I open the door and he says make us a tea, Joe. It's one of the very few times I ever see him without his lunch box. He actually looks like he's missing a limb. We've had a nice little earner son, he says. What you mean, I ask? I grabbed the two match boxes last night and took them to the Docklands and punted them a tenner a pop. Lunchbox I fuckin love ya you are a fuckin diamond. I owe you forever mate.

We split the money down the middle. I could pay Raymond plus have a bit left for me or that was my intention. A right little touch.

Later that night down The Partridge everyone's talking of how I'd run in the pub and thrown the two match boxes over the bar and everyone had turned the gaff upside down but no one could find them. Everyone was blaming everyone else. Even the cleaner got the blame.

I wait till me and Lunchbox are in the kharzi sharing a line of marching powder and having a piss and say did you tell anyone else that you found the matchboxes mate? Spence we go back years I've not told a soul. So I said let's just keep it between ourselves and see what happens but not a word can get out. Sweet Spence, he says.

The next afternoon Northern Jerry appears at the pub looking all smug and says I've come to pick you up to see Raymond cos you've fucked up dick head. In for a penny and all that. I thought right, I'll keep schtum and play it by ear. The drive was tense but I knew if needed I could pay

Raymond most of what I owed him and hopefully he'd see it as a good will gesture and maybe even give me a squeeze.

Once again I have to say I was most definitely a knob and constantly playing with fire. So I hear the acid went walkies in that shitty boozer the other night, Northern Jerry says. Raymond's going to find out who found them and I'm going to smash the fuck out of em. What you know, dick head? As much as you, I tell him. I was in the Old Bill station all night. You can't get a better alibi than that.

After about three quarters of an hour we pull up at Raymond's gaff and Jerry says you can go over the wall again if you want Dick head. No thanks Jer I reply sarcastically, in a country bumpkin accent. Slap round the head from Northern Jerry. Geezer can't take a gentle bit of ribbing. Fuckin arsehole I think but daren't say out loud. In we drive and are greeted by Ronnie who, for some reason always had a soft spot for me. Maybe she saw me as a younger man or something as she was a good fifteen years older than me, and if I'm being honest she was that ugly I'd have preferred it if Zeus the Doberman tried it on with me instead.

Hello Joseph, she says trying to charm me and I'm thinking if I was in trouble with the family maybe I best keep her onside. Cor you're looking as stunning as ever Ronnie I say with my biggest grin and most false look of lust. Shut up she says I'm far too old for you but as she says it she gently touches my cheek. Fuck me, imagine waking up next to that every morning is all I can think.

The twins appear, as alike as two proverbial peas in a pod. Fucking hell look what the cat dragged in says one of em, hope you've got our money says the other. Only family members could tell these two apart face to face whereas those of us not related had to accept their word when they introduced themselves. Though apparently Mason had a small birthmark on his lower back no-one ever had the arse to ask them to prove it.

Come in says Ronnie and take a seat we won't kill ya.

Jesus talk about put the spooks up me with a remark like that. I enter through the patio doors into a lovely big kitchen and am told to follow her through to the games room. She opens a door to a lavish gaff where Raymond and Curly are playing snooker on a full size table while Greg is sitting staring intently at a Rubik's cube trying to manipulate it to get all the colours matching but by the look in his moosh he's not having a lot of luck.

Hello young Joseph says Raymond what the fuck happened the other night? Fuck knows Ray. I mean Mr Fordham I say. I got chased and threw the acid tabs and my guess is some slippery fucker in the pub grabbed em or the Old Bill did and are keeping quiet about it.

"Well I have it on good authority the officers of the law most definitely do not have the said merchandise, Raymond says, and that's straight from the horse's mouth. So what are you going to do about my money young Joseph? I have two and half grand on me, Raymond, and I've got something in the pipeline that'll get me the rest as soon as possible. That young Joseph is a very good answer, I was expecting you to come here with some cock and bull story and pleading poverty but it's good to see you've made an effort to cover my losses.

All of a sudden there is a scream from the corner from Greg and the Rubik's cube goes flying into the wall and smashes apart, this fucking poxy pile of fucking shit is doing my nut in. As you have probably noticed I'm more often than not prone to say and speak stupid remarks before my brain has had a moment to actually process what my mouth is about to expel.

"Well you've royally fucked that up Gregg I say but at least you can put it all back together with it all in the right order and pretend you done it."

He charges at me like an American gridiron player and decks me. Before I know what's happening he's pinning me to the floor. He then grabs a yellow piece of his Rubik's cube and forces it into my mouth. Fucking hell. I've often wondered how I would finally leave this mortal coil and many strange options have come into my mind but never had it by choking on a Rubik's Cube being shoved down my throat by a gay psycho. I smacked him on the jaw as he forced the piece of Rubik's Cube into my mouth with Curly just standing there laughing his head off.

"See if you can put one of each colour down his throat Gregg" says Curly when in steams my knight in shining armour which in reality is my bulldog chewing a wasp deliverer from death, the most beautiful Veronica.

What the fuck you doing? She boots him full on the chin and he falls off me with a thud to the floor and then she grabs me and I think oh shit she's going to give me the kiss of fuckin life, come back and get on with it Gregg.

But no, she proceeds to kick me in the bollox. "Look what you've made me do to my little brother you prick."

I thought it prudent to say nothing at all and just curl up holding my crown jewels. Raymond pipes up and informs me he was on for a decent break before I came in so he decides to add another touch of insult to my injuries by slapping me around the face yet again.

Whole family's fucking mental.

As quick as it all started Greg gets up, cuddles Ronnie and says right Joseph would you like a tea or coffee? Fuckin hell who needs the twilight zone when you can just come round to Raymond's? Tea and a couple of pain killers please Gregg. Do you like it made in a pot with tea leaves mate he asks as if the last ten minutes had never occurred and we're old pals. Either way please mate maybe get me some ice for me nuts. Hahahahah he cracks up laughing and says she's off her rocker is our Ronnie.

I sit on a small leather chair as they all carry on like normal playing snooker and having a smoke. I get my tea in a bone china cup and saucer served like I'm in an exclusive restaurant by my personal waiter Greg. Joseph lets have that two and a half bags (bag of sand, grand). I say no worries but it's going to be in a bit of a mess thanks to Ronnie it's down me pants.

I begin pulling out rolled up piles of notes from me underwear and pass it on to Raymond who takes one look at it and says Greg take the money it's your fault it's got the smell of his bollocks and pubes all over it. Gregg don't bat an eyelid as he licks his finger and starts counting it out.

Two thousand five hundred and sixty pounds he says. Ahhh I'll have that tenner back I say to Greg. Fuck off he says you owe me that for my Rubik Cube, and he's in my face ready to finish me off - unlike the Rubik's Cube which he is never going to finish. Gregg calm the fuck down says Curly.

Gregg storms out slamming the door.

Jesus I've never wanted to get rid of a couple of grand so fast in me life and just get out of this madhouse while I'm still breathing.

Right you owe a grand and half now plus another half for the chaos you've caused in here. But Ray, I say, wanting to plead my case, when smack Curly punches me in the mouth and there goes the old Dracula fang and me lip starts bleeding. You know not to call him Ray, Curly kindly reminds me. Yeah I'm sorry for the trouble I've caused today, I tell Raymond. I'm just having a bad day I'll get your money as soon as I can Mr Fordham. Right off you go then young Joseph Raymond says holding out his hand for me to shake.

Shit do I shake it, I think, but I have no choice and clasp Raymond's hand.

Believe it or not I like you Joseph and I can tell our Veronica does as well so let's stay friends and don't mess me about again and I can see a bright future for you with our help. Thank you so much Mr Fordham I say, but thinking you can fuck right off and when you get there you can fuck off a bit more you lot are totally off the fuckin chart.

Just to complete the occasion in bowls Northern Jerry, shall I drop him back or feed him to Zeus he asks with a big grin on his face. Now now Jerry says Raymond don't be like that young Joseph is a good lad and is going to earn us a lot of money in the future, take him back and buy him lunch.

You couldn't make it up, I've gone from being the family punch bag to being taken for lunch by their paid goon. Off we go to Jerry's Granada Scorpio and out comes Ronnie to say bye. See you soon Joe she says, completely forgetting she nearly turned me into a eunuch half hour ago, and bends down and gives me a full on kiss forcing her tongue into me mouth. Oh my god she tastes like how I imagine roadkill tastes. For once I'm saved by my great friend Jerry, put him down Ronnie you don't know where he's been. Shut it you northern perv she tells him. I dive for cover in the back of his motor and slam the door.

Jerry jumps in and says where you want lunch dickhead? I tell you what Jer take me somewhere that does haggis so you can feel at home mate. I'm not your fuckin mate and I'm not fuckin Scottish dickhead. Okay, Wimpy Jer mate if you don't mind. Next time you call me Jer I swear I'm going to put your fuckin lights out.

So me and Jerry head off to the Wimpy and he parks outside without a second thought of the double yellow lines he's parked on. I order a Wimpy Grill and for dessert a Brown Derby and just cos Jerry is paying a Knickerbocker Glory. Greedy little fucker ain't ya he says ordering virtually the whole menu for himself. As we're sitting there Jerry suddenly jumps up and says fuckin cunt is giving me a ticket. I look out and a traffic warden is giving him a ticket on his pride and joy. Jerry is straight out and belts the poor bloke and when he hits the floor puts a few boots in for good measure.

Bloke is off his head.

He calls me through the window come on dickhead we've got to go, no thanks mate I'm staying here and finishing my Knickerbocker Glory. He speeds off in his car leaving the fella sprawled out on the roadside with people beginning to crowd round. Slippery fucker had done one without paying so I was left with the bill and had to convince the bloke I'd be back to clear it and for once in my life I stuck to my word on that one.

As I walked out after finishing up me Knickerbocker Glory an old girl's there declaring to the world she's written the number plate down on her shopping list and had a good description of the man and someone had run to the phone box to call the police. I was well chuffed. I'd had a really shit day but now I prayed Northern Jerry was going to get his collar felt.

In my opinion it couldn't happen to a better bloke.

The horrible fucker.

WHAT'S YOUR DATE OF BIRTH?

Jump forward to 2016 and the Joseph of the 80s and 90s is no more. Did I have a eureka moment or did I suddenly find religion? In truth, I don't know the one thing that made me realise I was going nowhere fast and life was passing me by in a drunken and stoned haze. I slipped up bad in the early 90s trying heroin for the first time while serving 90 days for a culmination of unpaid fines, and was chasing the dragon each and every day in a little cell with a fella called Jefferson. It took me out of those walls and soaring outside again and was an immense feeling, like nothing I'd ever experienced before.

I had built up fines for all manner of things, which to me were petty crimes but in reality were crimes nonetheless. Each time I'd get called to court I'd casually stroll in with just a duty solicitor for moral support and work my good old Joseph Spencer charm on all the magistrates. It would go something along the lines of Mr Spencer you are found guilty and the court fines you this amount while I'd stand there in my court attire of suit and tie looking like a respectable member of the community and would put on my most apologetic face and voice as I inform the three magistrates who held the key to my liberty in their hands that I have £50 pounds on me now but would need at least twenty of that because as soon as I walk out of court today I'm going out job hunting in the hope of turning my life around as I have fully seen the errors of my ways.

Somehow they always fell for it and would accept twenty or thirty pounds and the offer of a few quid each month and wish me luck in my hunt for employment. The old charm almost always stood me in good stead.

Almost.

By now The Duke had moved on from petty theft to robbing building society's fully armed. One day I'm sitting in The Bull - a big old pub - playing cards in the heart of the town centre when in comes The Duke calm as you like with a couple of plastic bags. He walks straight up and behind the bar and calls me over. I go behind the ramp and he leads me down to the cellar and immediately starts stripping off his clothes.

What the fuck Duke what's going on? Ask me nothing mate what you don't know can't get you in trouble. Fair enough and he then reaches in one of the bags, pulls out a massive wad and says wait a minute and goes out half-dressed and asks the governor to give him some change, preferably fivers. Do us a favour Joe go to Mister Byrites and get me some new clobber, everything pants and socks as well. No worries mate so off I troop into the shopping centre and notice a lot of Old Bill in the area, the real ones with the little caps and a few that were armed going in and out of the TSB building society.

I go in Byrites and in The Duke's size, which is much bigger than mine, I get him a complete new wardrobe still not knowing what's happened. It all gets paid and I have about forty pounds left thinking The Duke won't mind me keeping that. I go back in the pub down to the cellar and he's stark bollock naked. I give him what I've bought and he starts getting dressed. I say there's nearly a bullseye left mate can I bin it for helping you out. For the one and only time in his life The Duke raises his voice at me and says no you ain't having none of it. I say fuckin hell you've got bundles in that bag but he says Joe I'm doing you a favour mate just leave it.

So I go back to playing cards thinking fuckin hell even me oldest mate is turning on me. He comes out and buys everyone a drink and changes up loads of notes at the bar and has a game of cards. Jammy fucker ends up winning a couple of hundred quid in change off us all then says right I'm off, here you go you can have this change Joe and gives me all his winnings in coins.

He was always very clever was The Duke. He wouldn't give me any of the notes as it would've implicated me in the crime. It just so happened he'd calmly walked in the TSB with a shooter in one carrier bag and passed another over the counter telling them to fill it up with all the notes they had and then strolled out with nearly fourteen grand. He then walked hundred yards to The Bull, which is when I first saw him that day and had no inkling of what he'd done. The change he'd given me was simply that, change from a game of cards and in no way was me benefitting from his crime. I should never have doubted him. He was deliberately not telling me anything nor letting me have the notes from the building society.

A true friend.

The next day myself, The Duke and a young lady named Karen he had the hots for are walking from one pub to another when suddenly all hell breaks loose.

Cars pull up from every direction. Old bill of the flying squad kind all over us like a rash shouting on the floor now do not move put your hands on your head do not fuckin move. More shouting then we're all cuffed and sat up for everyone to stare at like exhibits in a museum.

All three of us are put in separate cars and taken to a nick in north London. We're all searched and thrown in cells and I am thinking fucking hell I was only going down the pub. I'm taken out of my cell and told I am under suspicion of aiding and abetting armed robbery. You're fuckin joking I say. When, where, armed with what?

A knock on the interview room door and in comes Mr Norman Wiseman in all his golden glory. Mr Wiseman was a top notch brief who was a thorn in the London and Essex and Kent constabulary's side, but no way could I afford him. I'd like a chat with my client please straight away and are you hungry Joseph? Very much, I say. Can we get my client a sandwich please and some privacy? They begrudgingly leave us alone together and he says I am Mr Raymond Fordham's brief and he heard you were in a predicament and told me to come and assist you at his behest. After all of our falling outs over money in the late 80s it had finally come to an end when I inadvertently saved his wife Val from being robbed while out and about.

Never one to see a woman bullied or threatened I was just sitting on a bench near a big park/common swigging a can of beer when Valerie Fordham pulled up and got out of her car with her grandson. A couple of shady looking fuckers made a beeline for Val and her necklace which was regal to say the least. One of them grabbed the little'un and the other threatened Val telling her what would happen to her and her grandson if she didn't take off her necklace and hand it over.

Val, as calm as you like, told them in no uncertain terms to disappear while they had the opportunity, and if the two fellas didn't clock then that perhaps this lady was connected then they were very, very thick. I ran up behind the one with the little grandson and smashed him full on round the head with my can of Holsten Pils. The other one looks at me and I give him the same.

Fucking wrong'uns targeting a lady and little kid. Their arse fell out big time and Val joined me in letting em have it while they were both on the deck. They scrambled up and were out of the park like the lowlife's they were. Joseph you little darling, she said, can you drive me home?

Sorry Val, I mean Mrs Fordham, correcting myself remembering all the clouts I get for calling her husband Ray, I can't drive.

She says well I'm too shook up so you'd better learn fast and get me home.

She sat the little'un in the back of her Volvo and she sat in the passenger seat with me in the driver's. I'd tried driving a couple of times and really couldn't get my head round the gears and the whole spacial awareness bit. I had a mate once try and get me to drive down some country lanes. it's a doddle, You'll piss it Joe he said.

So I was poodling down these lanes stuck in first gear with the engine roaring when Old Bill went past in the other direction giving us a look that says bonus I'm having them. We get round a bend in the road and I am unceremoniously grabbed from the front seat by a pal and the owner of the car swiftly jumps in the driver seat all the while lumps of gunja and joints are being hurled out the window. The Old Bill pull us and ask for the driver's details which are sweet and we're all searched and sent on our way.

I've watched a couple of mates get very long sentences for getting into so called road rage incidents and also know people who have been battered in similar incidents. It made me realise driving ain't for me. It seems to turn quite normal human beings into absolute lunatics, even mild mannered women tend to go wild once they get behind the wheel and shut the door. I can't drive and prefer to walk or get a bus or train.

I try half a dozen times to pull away in Val's Volvo but keep stalling, eventually managing to pull away with Valerie doing the gears for me.

Before I attempt to put it in second gear the Old Bill pulls up behind, blue lights flashing. Oh for fuck sake. I think I'm going to get done for driving offences now when two Old Bill jump out and run up to the car either side, I'm expecting to be dragged out by my hair but no, we're treated like royalty.

Mrs Fordham we had a call you were assaulted are you ok?

Yes, I'm fine young Joseph here saved me from two undesirables and I talked him into driving me home to my husband.

That's fine Mrs Fordham, they say, and well done Mr Spencer.

Fuckin hell, Old Bill are being nice to me. I must have slipped into a parallel universe. They couldn't be nicer to Val and at one point I'm thinking Jesus if they go any further up her arse they'll disappear. They agree that one of the officers will drive her home. I see this as my moment to vanish but Valerie ain't having none of it.

You are coming back with me. I'm going to tell Ray you saved mine but most importantly our little grandson from God knows what.

After the strangest journey back to the Fordham's gaff in the back talking to the little'un about school doing times tables with him while the copper asks Val if she got a look at either of them and would she be able to recognise them in a line up. No It all happened so quickly and I was in shock they could have been absolutely anyone, she says, and I'm sure Joseph couldn't help you either. No sorry I say, knowing full well that those two have chosen the most powerful lady in London apart from perhaps the Queen and Lady Di to try to rob and will be getting a visit soon and a serious pasting after which they'll be wishing that they'd got nicked for it instead.

We get back and Raymond rushes out what the fuck he screams at the copper grabbing his grandson from the back seat without giving me a second glance. You can be as hard as nails but everyone has a weak spot.

Raymond's were Val and his grandson.

The place looked different without Northern Jerry giving it the big'un but he was currently banged up for murdering the traffic warden outside the Wimpy a couple of years previous. Not murder exactly. Not at the time, anyway. He never passed away until a couple of months later and Jerry got twelve years. Pity he didn't get life. He is a seriously dangerous and damaged human being, while the poor traffic warden died a slow death with his pregnant wife by his side. A large amount of money was posted through her door anonymously shortly after he died and most people knew it was from Raymond.

Greg makes us all a brew. In we go and the copper is told in no uncertain terms that the only involvement the police were to have is to find out one or both of the names of the two unluckiest would-be robbers in London. Yes, Mr

Fordham, as soon as we know we'll call you straight away. And with his tail between his legs the copper was off to his colleague waiting at the gates.

Where does Joseph fit in here Val? Val tells Raymond of my heroic deed. She plays up my part till I felt like Charles Bronson - a true life vigilante. It was nothing Mr Fordham, I say, I did what anyone would have done. Joseph I owe you big time, if there's ever anything you need you know where I am, now I want to spend time alone with my wife. He called me a taxi and as I was about to leave Val gives me a massive hug and the little grandson comes out and gives me a cuddle and a drawing which he told me was a superhero (me) beating up two bad guys. I was truly moved.

Right your cab will be at the gates, Joseph. Tell him to put it on my bill. Thank you Mr Fordham, I say having learned my lesson but he calls me back and gives me a massive bear hug and says after today young Joseph you can call me Ray. Fuckin hell, I think, after a dozen slaps and digs I can call him Ray. Again my usual self of speaking words that form in my brain before I have processed them I say nice one Raymondo. I await the slap but he just looks at Val and says more front than Sainsbury's this one, Val.

WHAT'S YOUR DATE OF BIRTH - PART TWO?

So Mr Spencer it seems that they are trying to implicate you in something you know absolutely nothing about, am I correct? Completely correct Mr Wiseman. Quite simply, Mr Spencer, they have no evidence at all and your friend Mr Dukes has admitted his guilt and you and the young lady should both be released shortly. You are to give no comment at all. Yes, Mr Wiseman.

As always Mr Norman Wiseman was bang on the money and me and Karen were released without charge within a couple of hours but The Duke was up the swanny big time.

Back to the non-payment of fines court hearing and I'm expecting the same as usual. While this had been going on The Duke had been going back and forwards for hearings at the magistrate's court before eventually being sentenced at crown court to a big old chunk of bird.

Knowing he was up in the same court on the same day I travelled up with his lovely old mum Jean. She was like a second mum to me. Jean would sit briefly on The Duke's hearing then hoped the court would let her pop down and briefly visit him while I would get my usual slapped arse, then I was going to buy her some lunch. Sadly, that day went as far from to plan as it is possible to go.

As I'm in the dock giving it the usual spiel it suddenly dawns on me things don't seem to be going how I thought they would. The magistrate in the middle of the three starts waffling numbers at me 15 days, 12 days, 20 days. I'm thinking what's he on about and say to the duty solicitor what's all that about he says they've given you so and so many days. Mr Spencer, says the middle magistrate, you have had ample time to pay these fines and repeatedly failed to do so and keep churning out excuse after excuse and we feel you consider it all a game of harmless fun. Well you have to learn that the fines were all imposed for offences you were found guilty of. Take him down. Bollocks. That weren't meant to happen. And fucking hell its nearly Christmas. I don't want to be banged up over Christmas.

I'm taken down to the couple of dozen or so cells down below in the bowels of the court and see the name Dukes chalked on the little board on one of the cell doors. I say can I go in with him, he's an old friend? No but you can say hello, these are all single down here. He opens the flap and The Duke is sitting there reading a book. He looks up from his wooden graffiti covered bench and says Spence I'm surprised they let you down for a visit, they gave me mum a hard time. She said you're taking her for some lunch. I said I've just got 90 days' mate just before Christmas I'm fuckin gutted. The Duke being him burst out with his unmistakable hearty laugh. Cheers mate I say as the screw shows me to my cell.

After ten minutes The Duke shouts oi Spence press your buzzer and tell that gaoler I've got a little parcel for you he's sweet as, mate. So I buzz and he duly opens the flap on my door and I inform him that Dukes has something for me. He walks over and collects a big A4 size envelope and inside is some tobacco, a lump of puff, some rizla, a few Swan Vesta matches and a pack of playing cards. Cheers guv I say to the gaoler.

End of the day it makes his life easier to turn a blind eye to things and let people have a joint as it calms things down. Back then you could still smoke in cells. I roll and light a joint and just start to chill out when The Duke throws a spanner in the work as he shouts oi Spence I've just fell in, you're 21 now you're going to go to proper nick and I'm still at Feltham on remand. Oh fuck, instant paranoia kicks in. I think back to the first time I walked in Lambeth and grabbing on to Dee for all I was worth in order not to get taxed of my trainers and belongings, how was I going to cope in there on me own and then going to a bloke's adult nick.

He shouts it's simple, mate, add a year on your date of birth and you'll come to Feltham with me and I can look after you. So back then at the end of each day's proceedings a Sweatbox would turn up next to the court and one at a time you would all be handcuffed and led to the waiting wagon, be asked name and date of birth and then lobbed in a little compartment and they'd put your name in chalk on the door and what nick you were going to after you get to Lambeth.

I go up and he says name? Joseph Spencer I say. Date of birth and I just add a year onto my date of birth - 69 instead of 68. Bosh how easy was that. He throws me in my little Sweatbox within the Sweatbox and shortly up comes The Duke. He gives his details and as he walks past gives me a wink. Once the screw went to get someone else he said sorted Spence it says Feltham on your door. Result. I'll go there and be in the company of The Duke so if it goes tits up I've got back up on a grand scale cos by then he was virtually invincible.

The long drive again but being late December it was dark outside and once again I prayed to all the gods for divine intervention and sobbed quietly once again as I watched the world go by. Christmas lights were up all over London and it was heart-breaking to think I was going to face Christmas behind a door and wall.

WHAT'S YOUR DATE OF BIRTH = PART THREE?

After a torturous journey we reach Lambeth and I'm getting prepared for the forthcoming ambush for when the cell door opens, but at least this time - just like the last - I've got someone who can and will look after me and I know what to expect. Or so thought I hear a few getting unloaded then as my door is unlocked the screw says we seem to have a discrepancy with your date of birth and I'm thinking shit what do I do now.

I repeat the same as earlier with a year added on and he says it says here on official papers you were born in 68? Are you thick don't you know when your birthday is? I tell him again the wrong answer and am told you're going to have to go in a little holding cell for half hour while we check the paperwork. The Duke gives me a wink from his little piece of sweatbox and crosses his fingers for me, and that was the last I would see of him until I go visit him about a year on.

I'm thrown in a cell and Hallelujah there's only one little black fella laid out on the bench on his own, thank fuck, so no ambush. I introduce myself and the manor I'm from going through the ritual of who, what and why I'm here and he nods and says I'm Felix from New Cross.

I shake his hand and we're sitting there chatting and he says I'm surprised they put you in with me mate to be honest. I'm thinking that's a silly thing to say then get paranoid thinking shit maybe he's a mass murderer or something and innocently ask him why and he says calm as you like cos I've got AIDS. Fucking hell, that's the gay thing they're all dying of.

I move as far away from him as possible and press the buzzer to escape what I think's a certain death sentence as I'm breathing the same air he's breathing out. I try holding my breath and keep pressing the buzzer. Back then we really didn't understand how it was transmitted and believed the bullshit that simply being in a room with someone was contagious. He said I caught it from a dirty syringe I've got a bird and kids and no bloke's ever been near my arse.

The door opens and I say you're right I had my date of birth wrong cos I was in shock you need to get me out of this cell. I've often wondered what happened to Felix. The poor bloke had a bad habit and it sadly gave him a terrible disease, a disease which in later years would and could be treated. I hope he was and that he went on to live a perfectly normal life.

I am told, seeing as I'm 21, I will be going to Penton Ville - the 'Ville so I'm led back in to a cell and the door is opened and I await the incoming onslaught that is surely on the horizon, but nothing. There are about 20 or so blokes ranging from early 20s to late 60s sat all round quietly chatting. Alright son says the bloke next to me says and we start chatting. He's Richie and he's got 7 years for robbery. Slowly we all reveal our names and sentences and they're all upwards of at least a couple of years and when I say Joseph 90 days for non-payment they all burst out laughing. I'm informed by them all it's a doddle and I'll be out before I even have time for a shave. Joints are then rolled and shared around.

Completely different to the under 21 cells where I now understand - being young lads - everyone in there's trying to impress each other and find their place in the pecking order whereas these are all old cons and have nothing to prove to anyone. I thought about throwing Raymond's name out there as a bit of protection but just thought it better to keep quiet as they might think who's this soppy little fucker. After a while three of us are told our sweatbox is awaiting our presence so we say our cheerio's to the others and off we go on the short trip across London from Lambeth to Penton Ville. Ends up it's not a sweatbox at all just a little van where we're all cuffed to a seat. Once again looking out at all the Christmas lights is a proper wakeup call that I have regally fucked up and this is real and my arse is going to be locked up over xmas.

We arrive at the big foreboding walls of the 'Ville and an army of screws who, for some reason, refuse to take us. Turns out they're striking about something or other and not accepting anyone new. After a lot of toing and throwing they say we can stay for the night but will have to be picked up early the next day to be dispatched elsewhere. Nothing like Mr T greets us just an old lag offering us a burn. Each of us is then welcomed with a strip search and a gloved finger up the arse then a shower and prison garb.

I'm lobbed in a grimy little cell on A wing first night induction unit. I struggle to sleep worrying where I'm going to be shipped to the next day. After a shit night I'm woken early and told to go and change back into my own clothes I'm off to Highbury Vale. Never heard of it. It's a large Old Bill station on the Blackstock Road and you'll be there till you get allocated elsewhere. So off I go in a car this time on my own handcuffed to a copper in the back, though after a couple of minutes he fully understands I have no intention of trying to do a runner and undoes the cuffs and we chat about life and football and women and movies. He asks if I'd seen a recent movie - Goodfellas. I said it's about a grass ain't it? and we both laugh.

We arrive at Highbury vale and I'm taken in and once more strip searched and I calmly tell the copper I've just come straight from the 'Ville with one of your lot and he jokingly says exactly we`re the biggest gang in London as he rifles about up me backside. I see the names on a board of those in the cells and see a certain number cell and it says Webster "escapee" next to it and think don't put me with him for fuck sake. Like he can read my fuckin mind the copper says put him in twelve with Webster. Oh you've got to be winding me up. The door is unlocked and laying on one of the benches/beds is a big black fella spark out for the count. Jeff wake up you've got someone to keep you company. He opens his eyes looks at me like he's literally going to eat me for breakfast, but then offers his hand and says Jefferson Webster welcome to my humble abode.

I shake his hand and introduce myself and tell him I've got 90 days' blah blah blah and the Ville wouldn't except us cos of a screw strike. He says he's been here on his jacks for a couple of weeks and doesn't beat around the bush telling me he's addicted to heroin and asked if I want a chase. All the smack heads I'd ever encountered seemed ill looking yet this was a big old lump and considering the lack of daylight he was getting in the cell looked really well. He says you are allowed a visit every three days, you've had a right result ending up here, and no one watches you on the visits and showed me his stash of smack, silver foil Rizla fags and a massive lump of puff. He tells me he's a registered user and each night they give him a couple of pills that knock him clean out and if I want anything feel free to take it. I ask about the escapee on board outside and this is how it went.

He was doing 3 years and going to an outside hospital for something or other but took the two screws hostage with an old style toothpaste tube that was equivalent to a shit sharp razor. He managed to get out of the vehicle and was on the run for a couple of days where he went and had his leg over with a lady of the night before giving himself up. He takes a break from his story and has a chase of the dragon offering me a go to which I inform him never ever over my dead body. Fair enough he says but it makes the days a lot better. Wallop he's gone just like that and there's a really strong smell of vinegar which tells me he's using black tar smack which is mixed with all sorts of shit. I decide to have a joint off his lump of hash instead.

The cell door is opened and I think fuck they're going to smell it but the copper doesn't bat an eyelid. Come on then while Jeff's asleep it's time for a walk and I'm taken to the car park where two coppers take it in turns to walk round and round with me while I get some exercise. I'm taken back to the cell where Jeff is still soundo and given a dinner and told lights will be off at nine so if I wanted to read hurry up. Fair enough. I grab a Stephen King book from Jeff's collection and choose *The Talisman*. It's about a world in another dimension where we all have a doppelganger and it hooked me instantly.

A massive 600 odd pages, that book helped me kill many a dark hour as it transferred my mind beyond the cell walls and the door and the lock that held me here.

Like I said, Jeff was out for the night. We got to know each other well over the next couple of days but on Christmas Eve I had a meltdown when it really hit home that I was stuck here for Christmas. Jeff explained that next Christmas this would all be a distant memory whereas for him he faced at least the next five Christmases behind a door. But that really didn't help me and that Christmas Eve was the day I first tried heroin. Not a day or moment that should be rejoiced but at that time I saw no other way to get me through. He got my chase prepared, placing the shit on a piece of foil and heating it up then holding it for me to inhale with a small straw.

And I was gone.

Fuck me, Christmas Day I wake up absolutely slaughtered with a pounding headache and feeling sick as a dog. The coppers on duty at lunch time bring us in a full on Christmas dinner and even a cracker to pull trying to make it as normal as possible. They were decent coppers; much better than most proper screws I'd encountered. Me and Jeff then decided to have another chase to celebrate Christmas and before I know what's happening Christmas Day was over. Each night after that Jeff would get his pills which would knock him out and I began having a little chase while he was asleep.

Early January I get a visit off my mum. I was stoned and it frightened the life out of her and she left in a bad way which made me have another little go. Shit, without realising it I soon couldn't get through the day without a bit of smack.

I've since read up and spoken to educated people on the subject and heroin causes the body to release dopamine which gives you that great rush that you get at first but severe drowsiness for hours afterwards.

A few days after my mum came up I'm told I have a visit and walk into the little interview room where a table and two chairs were placed for visits and sitting there is Raymond and Valerie Fordham. You look fuckin awful young Joseph I hope you ain't being a silly boy. I think thanks Mr Fordham nice to see you too but say nothing cos I just feel embarrassed. I hadn't washed for a good few days, I just couldn't be bothered and me and Jeff just lay there stoned day and night anyway. Nice to see you Mrs Fordham I say and she gives me a hug and says Joseph your mum got in touch she's worried about you. I owe you Joe and don't want you getting involved in any nonsense. I'm fine, I lie. Bollocks says Raymond, you stink and look like shit you're on the gear. Wallop another of Raymond's slaps straight round the moosh. if you've come here to slap me then I'm going back to my cell I say and storm out. I hear a lot of commotion from the room but go back to my cell and get on Jeff's earhole for a little piece of gear, but he ain't had a visit and is out of everything.

The door opens and Jeff is told he has a visit. He's gone half hour and I'm pissed off. After a while back he comes and I'm hoping he's got a parcel and first thing he says is you never told me Raymond Fordham looks after you. I say he don't, he always gives me a dig when I see him. Well unfortunately mate it's over you're being moved to a cell on your own, Raymond just explained what's what mate and if I give you anything at all he's going to find out and I'll be totally fucked. sorry mate. As simple as that it was done and I was lobbed in a cell on my own. Raymond had told him in no uncertain terms not to give me anything at all and that was that. Raymond's power reached beyond walls and doors.

I take my small collection of books and for the next five weeks I'm all on my own, apart from the books and a radio. Raymond and Valerie come back a couple of times and while Ray's outside Val explains that Ray didn't want me touching all that drug shit. She says you look like the lovable little Joseph again with a twinkle in your eye, rather than a paranoid mess. Raymond comes in, gives me a firm handshake and says if you ever touch that shit again I'll batter ya. You have a lovely mum, he goes on, so don't you dare put her through that. He tells me he'd let her know I was okay and to come back up to visit. I had by then had many slaps from Ray and his family as well as a few boots in the nuts but deep down he was a decent bloke who in his own strange way sort of liked me.

When I walked out of Highbury Vale I knew no way would I ever touch that shit again. I thought it helped me through a dark period but in fact it just made things much worse and made me rude to the one person in the world who would give the very air they breathe for me - my mum. I owe Raymond big time and I am proud to say both him and Valerie are great friends now, Ray being in his early 70s but still as imposing as ever. He doesn't slap me anymore and will always listen to me when I speak what with that being now part of what I do. I give motivational speeches and also go to school's colleges etc. talking to the pupils about all sorts and the perils of living a stupid life, I also work part time in a library.

Jefferson Webster sadly passed away of an overdose a few days after his release after serving five more Christmas days behind a door, but not before he had a final leg over with a lady of the night.

He looked after me and was a good man.

God bless you, Jeff.

JEWISH JACK IS A CATHOLIC!

Jack came out after a large chunk of bird and within a few months the poor bastard was diagnosed with prostate cancer. He came out drug free and looked a picture of health. He had a spring in his step and I would bump into him now and again on the manor but by then I was living a totally different life, I didn't touch anything stronger than a drop of vodka with a drop of lemonade and tried to distance myself from the people and the lifestyle that I fully recognised as being bad for me mentally. I have still not touched a drug apart from prescribed ones from the chemist and, of course, the chemotherapy which helped save my life.

I now appreciate the beauty all around me in everyone and everything and do not need to be chemically enhanced to do that. Once Jack was diagnosed he was fitted with a bag to piss in and deteriorated rapidly being drawn back to heroin and crack. I chatted to him several times and his attitude was I served all that fuckin time, got clean and then get cancer, what's the point?

I couldn't really argue with him to be honest.

By the early 2000s I'd met Abbie. She came up to me in the library where I work and asked me if anyone was available who could help her with a CV. I helped her with her CV and she thanked me and left telling me she was going for an interview the following day. I wished her luck, not expecting to see her again. A couple of days later she comes back in and tells me she got the job and would I like to have a drink with her to celebrate? Off we go and I have to say I was smitten by her instantly. She could read me like a book off the shelf in my own library.

To this day I can't lie to her as it would upset her, which in turn would upset me, so no matter what I am honest with her. We have our children as well our darling granddaughter who has us both wrapped around her finger. The first time I held that little bundle I finally understood what life was all about.

It all comes down to this, your child having a child and DNA passing along the line so no matter what you will exist in one form or other long after your physical being has departed this life. It was my granddaughter who I focused on when I was diagnosed with cancer of the bowel in 2018. She was just a baby and had no idea of who I was or what she meant to me and it gave me a goal that no way was this little girl going to grow up without knowing how much I love her. I carried a photo of her in my pocket to each scan and planted a mental image of her at the front of my mind each appointment with the great oncology team who saved my life.

Sadly, I had lost two of my sisters to the same disease and my great mum had to bury two of her babies, which no parent should ever do. This crushed her but she still battled on for many years, though part of her was always with her girls. I made up as much as I could for the troubles I had constantly brought to her door over the years but I always remained her little Joseph.

My Abbie became a surrogate daughter to her and they got on so well it was like Abbie appeared not just for me but for Mum also. I had grown up a spoilt little brat who could never do wrong in the eyes of my mum and sisters and they also went through so much from our dad.

As I said earlier he was a vicious man who would drink then assault them all. They were all older than me and had to endure it as well as protecting their little brother from it all. My maternal nan passed away on Christmas day when I was just a baby so I never knew her, nor my maternal grandad. She was a Russian immigrant who'd escaped the Russian revolution in her teens all on her own. She somehow made her way to England when back then it was so difficult to get from country to country.

That's why I will never jump on those who come here searching for a better life cos I would not be here now if she hadn't made that journey. I never even knew my paternal grandparent's names only that my dad's mum would actually assist him in the beatings of my mum. Absolutely vile people of the worst type.

I comprehend now how hard it would have been for Mum each year on Christmas Day trying to make sure her kids were happy even though it was the anniversary of her own mum's passing. But happy is what she made us. Never once did she let her own grief get in the way of her children having a great Christmas. She would work several jobs at a time to make ends meet. She'd often collect me from school when I was about 5 or 6 and had a job in a launderette and get me a comic usually - Beano or Dandy - and a little jamboree bag of sweets that'd keep me quiet for a few hours in the laundrette while she washed and folded everyone's washing to earn a few pounds to make ends meet and put food on the table. To this day the smell of a laundrette transports me back to the time when everything seemed safe and I'd sit there with a comic eating black jacks and fruit salads, Mum having her favourite Parma Violets while studiously folding a total stranger's clothes.

She would often say she wasn't hungry but now I figure that was probably because there wasn't enough food to go around. She would go hungry just so we could eat.

I would walk down the road with Mum, clinging to her hand knowing full well nothing could get to me while she was with me. I like to think in her later life she felt the same way about her little Joseph when me and Abbie took to caring for her. Even then she worked sewing hooks and eyes onto clothes and sat at a sewing machine for hours on end repairing clothes for friends and neighbours.

There was a time Mum worked serving the school dinners at my school. I had a right result as she would give me and The Duke massive scoops of everything. We were fed well while she worked there and would always be back for seconds. For a number of years, she also worked with people with learning difficulties and they all absolutely worshipped her. It was when she had this job I grasped how lucky I had been in the great race of life.

I could not have chosen a better person to be my mum, I truly couldn't have. I was blessed to not only have a great mum but also sisters who, in their own ways, were like extra mums - and looked after me no matter what mess I got in. So many people have come into my life who have nothing but my best interests at heart.

No drug can replicate that feeling of being loved.

I cannot and do not preach about never using drugs. We all have our own demons and we all have our breaking point. And someone can only stop using when *they* want to, not when a loved one wants them to. I've known all sorts who've slipped into a life consisting of deal after deal, buzz after buzz. I have known - and still know - females who sell themselves for money to feed a habit. They don't do it cos they enjoy getting fucked by total strangers they do it cos it is a means to an end - pure and simple. All the time they're out there they're putting themselves in danger of all kinds, generally with a bloke somewhere in the shadows not only taking half of what they earn but then supplying them with gear. It's a vicious circle.

All addicts are somebody's child and deserve a break. They are human beings who just chose a wrong turn at some point in their life.

That's all. They're not *bad* people.

And the people you see begging sitting outside shops are also somebody's little Joseph. Circumstances led them to this point. They need help but many don't know how to ask for it.

There but for the grace of God go the rest of us. That is why I try never to judge.

I would randomly bump into Jewish Jack out and about and each time he looked worse than the time before. He was bang on it again and looked like he was due a Christmas card from the queen, he looked skeletal. He was in and out of hospital for his cancer and all whilst also being in and out of crack dens. He was simply existing. What happened to the fiery bastard who shot me in the shin and give me a hiding for garden hopping for fuck sake? He was married and divorced and had a couple of kids he rarely saw.

His son would turn up at odd times and beg and ponce off his dad who had fuck all to ponce. The lad was falling into the same lifestyle.

I would spend hours talking to Jack at his elderly parents' house sitting in the kitchen trying to make him eat some toast and have a cup of tea but he would disappear in the garden and come in smashed and fall asleep and I would carry him up to his bed, lay him in the recovery position and leave.

Abbie wanted me to stop seeing Jack as it was wearing me out mentally but for all his faults as well as our falling outs he was a man at death's door. I couldn't desert him. Abbie has an attitude so similar to mine whereby she doesn't see the bad in people. she was just worried I'd slip into my old way. But seeing Jack made me even more convinced that wasn't the life for me.

I get a phone call one morning. By then the majority of people had a mobile though they were just going from massive bricks to the newer tiny little Nokia type. I was told by my mate Dale that Jack had been rushed into hospital a few days previous and had sadly passed away. I was gutted. Absolutely gutted. But it was inevitable. Jack had simply given up.

People asked me when the funeral was but as far as I was aware Jewish people were buried straight away, so it had been and gone. I thought I'd pay my respects and pop and see Jack's very elderly mum and dad, Iris and Stan. I knocked and a carer who was looking after them opened the door and Iris shouted let him in. I walk in the front room, pretty much by then the whole universe for this old couple, they had a commode and everything they needed was done by a carer. God knows what they had made of Jack.

I say I'm so sorry about Jack is there anything I can do. No we're fine Joe, says Iris, he's better off now, he died the day he first touched that shit. Older people have a way of hitting the nail flush on the head so I just nod and say how did the funeral go? Old Stan - forever the old cockney - chirps up fuckin hell Joe he's only been gone a few days he ain't even cold yet. Sorry Stan I just thought Jews were buried straight away. What makes you think he's Jewish, Stan says? I say everyone calls him Jewish Jack - even you do Iris. Hahahahhaha they both burst out laughing. He ain't Jewish, Joe, Iris says, he's a Catholic.

They tell me a teacher shouted hey you when he was first year of juniors and half the class burst out laughing mistakenly thinking he called him hey Jew, and from there he was known as Jewish Jack and the name just stuck. Well fuck me sideways. After saying my goodbyes, I had to ring The Duke to let him know as him and Jack had been pals and also served time and earnt money together.

I ring him and straight away he says did they say the funeral went off ok? I say guess fuckin what Jewish Jack's a catholic. What you on about he says and I tell him the score. Even in Jack's death there was humour as there also was when we finally got to go to his funeral. Me and The Duke were letting as many people know as possible guess what Jewish Jack's a Catholic and his funeral is such and such time and place. But Jack had upset many people and no one was interested in going.

Whatever someone does they deserve a decent send off. In the couple of weeks building up to Jack's funeral I found out from his parents they'd been giving him money each week to pay for his and their funerals but he'd been jacking it up instead. Quite a few quid, in all. His poor parents now were worried not just about their son's funeral costs but also their own as neither wanted to leave the other with a debt. I'm glad to say myself and Raymond managed to put that right before it was ever needed.

Ray had buried his own son, also called Raymond. Little Raymond born in1983 and killed close to his 30th birthday. He was a charming young man who went to a private school and had not a single aggressive bone in his body. He was out with work mates from the city, he was involved in the stock market and had been invited for a drink to celebrate turning 30. An argument ensued in a bar and a knife was pulled out and he was stabbed through the heart. He was nothing like his dad or uncles and never threw the name about as he could have. He was a bright individual in his own right and his passing blew a massive hole in the lives of the whole family, but it hit big Ray extra hard. I felt their pain and when I went to him and explained about the predicament Jewish Jack's parents were in he fronted the money immediately and told me not to tell them where it came from.

Their other son Clinton was in and out of prison and a bit of a let-down to his parents despite the private schooling he had. He wanted to be a gangster but the world had changed since his old man's day and London, Kent and Essex was now being swallowed up by eastern Europeans and Russians who would wipe you out in an instant with no second chances. He got involved in a deal that went arse up and got a 7-year sentence.

JEWISH JACK IS A CATHOLIC! - PART TWO

Me and The Duke met on the morning of Jewish Jack the Catholic's funeral and got a train and a bus to the crematorium/cemetery. The train went according to plan but the bus took forever, finally grinding to a halt about a mile or so from the crematorium/cemetery gates. We look out of the front of the bus and there's a massive funeral on its way and the pall bearers were doing a very slow walk leading a long procession.

Fuckin hell, d'ya reckon that's for Jack? says The Duke. No way mate, I say. We ask the driver to let us off the bus but being a stubborn jobsworth sort he tells us no it's not a bus stop. I sense The Duke is about to explode. Oh fuckin hell mate he says we're going to a fuckin funeral. I press the little button and we both jump off while the driver gives us the finger for daring to want to get to a funeral on time.

We sprint off down the road. I say 'sprint' but there's me now with arthritis in my hips and legs and a slight limp thanks to Jack thinking he was a cowboy and shooting me all them years back, and The Duke in front of me out of breath cos he smokes like a trooper. I've also got shoes on that've got a metal quarter tip on the bottom making me slip everywhere. We get to the cortege and try to quietly walk past. We quickly see it wasn't for Jack. It's a soldier's funeral with many of the mourners in the cars dressed up in their uniforms. Just as we get past The Duke has a coughing fit and pukes up a huge amount of phlegm. We get overtaken by the cortege and decide we're too old for this running lark and start walking, hoping to make it in time.

When we get there the soldiers are getting out of the cars and are making a big circle for the coffin so we figure out that'll be in the crematorium and Jack's going to be buried in the cemetery. We run up and push the door of the little chapel but its locked. Shit we're too late. Who you looking for gents asks a grave digger. The funeral of Jack Parsons, mate. He says nope I've seen today's list and there's no-one of that name. He must be in the small chapel. Where's that mate? Just past the soldiers there's a little door round the side. So off we go again and as we hit the road after coming off the grass I slip on my fuckin quarter tips in the middle of all the soldiers as they're unloading the coffin.

I lay there in a heap. The Duke does what he always does and bursts out laughing. He then scoops me up like a little doll, apologises to all and carries me off. We charge through the small chapel door, and its empty. Bollox we really have missed it. As we're walking back out, from a little side room we hear Iris say is that you Joseph? We go in and there's Iris, Stan, Jack's ex-wife and a couple who look like they are on gear. And that's it. Neither of his kids even bothered turning up.

We finally go in and say a final farewell to Jewish Jack. I speak on behalf of his parents and as a friend and we all solemnly trudge out into the crisp September air. The two strangers ask if there's a wake and is there food and drink laid on and when told no they disappear into the sunset. Obviously just a couple of smack or crack heads who thought they'd see what was up for grabs.

His parents go home with Jack's ex, while the duke and myself head back to the bus stop. When the bus pulls up it's the same jobsworth from earlier who refuses to open the door and drives off, leaving us standing there. What an absolute bell end. So we walk back, and just like when we were kids we laugh at everything and everyone we see, taking the piss and just being as we once, were. We parted that day with his usual I love you Joseph Spencer. He always told me he loved me and he is one of the few males I would say that to and mean it.

If only then I knew The Duke was struggling mentally and would in the not distant future take his own life.

After coming out from being on remand and pleading guilty just to be free again, I had some probation to do. I met my officer and was informed that I along with eleven others had been selected for a trial. This was the beginning of what a few years later made headlines in the tabloids when young offenders were sent away abroad as part of their punishment and the public were rightfully up in arms.

Ours wasn't quite abroad - unless you class Wales as abroad. Me and a good mate of mine - Terry - he who did the front crawl on the pavement outside Buck House - arrived together and were introduced to the others at the newly built probation offices in the town centre. We all immediately got on and the first week we just sat in a room with a few officers talking.

One officer called Phillip, another called Peter and a beautiful posh young lady called Julie. All of us just clicked. We were told every other week, instead of just reporting to the probation service, we would do some form of activity as well as the weekend in Wales. Harsh punishment or what.

So one week a 1 to 1 with either Philip, Peter or Julie, the next all of us together causing mayhem. I had to sit with Julie the first week and she really knew how to use her good looks in order to get me to open up. I found I could talk and tell her things I didn't even understand myself. For the very first time she made me look hard at the lifestyle I led, and pretty quickly told me I did it because I just tried to fit in rather than being a loner, and that was my biggest downfall.

Although it made sense to me it took many more years for me to fully comprehend and take the action needed to change my ways and turn my life full circle. The second week we all met up we were told we were going canoeing at an activity centre.

Wahey off we go.

All in a van together, singing at the top of our voices. the three officers singing along with us. A proper strange old turnout indeed.

The first morning in Wales we're given a canoe and some bloke is telling us the ropes but we're all blanking him taking not an iota of interest in what he's saying. Off we all go steaming about capsizing each other and going mental, then in comes Phillip and Julie. She had a skin tight wetsuit on and we're all wolf whistling and behaving like dogs on heat.

As soon as Phillip hits the lake we assault him with our canoes from every direction like bumper cars. In the water he goes, to cheers from us all. Even Julie has a chuckle. Poor old Phil. On another occasion we're taken ten pin bowling. We're all sneaking outside to have a puff on a joint and generally misbehaving like the little shits we are. We had a competition of who could smash the lights in the ceiling with a bowling ball.

Phillip, Peter and Julie would always, without fail, try to get us to open up why we behaved in certain ways. Instead of shouting at us they ask what's on our mind, what are we thinking and does it make you feel good. It's a strange approach but they stuck to it rigidly.

Another time we're taken to Dover Castle for some reason. We spend half the day stuck in traffic then the rest of the day looking round the castle, and on the way back they stop and buy us all McDonalds. You have to remember this is a punishment from the courts of the land. Fuck knows who was paying for it. We all got grub and milk shakes and extra straws along with serviettes to use as mouth darts.

We're all in the van chewing bits of the napkin and sending them flying damp and soggy through the end of a straw. Silly boys we most certainly were. We pull up at a set of traffic lights and there's a few rocker type fellas on big motorbikes sitting there. The van's got these little slide type windows you can open a fraction so a couple of us open the window for a clear shot and bomb the geezers on the bikes straight in the face with the soggy tissue. NO visor on these bad boys, just a crash lid and that was it.

Fuck me they went mental. One jumped straight off his bike and charged at the van. Quick Pete pull away that mad fucker's going to kill us. Peter took one look and floored it across the lights and for a few miles these bikers were chasing the probation officers and a rowdy bunch of late teens. Once we cleared them we decide to start launching pillows about. These were added luxury bought along for our comfort but suddenly going down the motorway we're throwing them all round the van till one hits Pete and he nearly loses the van.

He eventually pulled over and we were all expecting a bollocking but instead we're all asked what was you thinking, what went through your mind, did we realise the consequences our actions could have caused? Proper fuckin weird. We got to know these three very well and all were good people trying to do the pretty impossible job of taming rabid little shits like us. They would unwittingly lend us money under the pretence of needing to go out job hunting but instead we spent it down the pub.

There was a time myself and Terry genuinely decided we were going to go and look for a job but needed money for a travel card and also to have our photos taken for something or other in one of those little booths. At this time, we were still on bail for another offence and part of the conditions of the bail were we couldn't go within certain boundaries of the town centre apart from when we had to visit the probation office.

So me and Terry head to the office and explain to Julie that we need some money for the photos etc. and she willingly lends us the money which she knows full well she will never get back. Now we have two options, we can travel about four miles to another area and get the photos done or go into the centre we're banned from. As we're standing there debating whether it's worth the risk of having our bail revoked, up pull two of our protagonist coppers.

What you two doing here, you're not meant to be here? We tell them the what, why and where of what we plan on doing and they say tell you what seeing as you're going to look for a job we'll turn a blind eye and you can go to Woolworths and we'll overlook it. Nice one we think, and off we go to Woollies.

At Woolies we go straight to the photo booth. Terry's going in to have two photos done then I'm going to jump in for two - or that's the plan. He has his, I jump in and pull the curtain back across, and sit on the little round stall and as the booth flashes I hear outside, what you doing here you're breaking your bail! Terry starts arguing giving it bollocks you just told us we could come in here. Then I see the unmistakable sight a couple of pairs of Old Bill Dr Martens under the curtain. The curtain's pulls open and straight away one of the slippery fuckers says I'm arresting you for breach of bail, and immediately cuffs me. Terry jumps out and starts kicking off sending stuff flying off of shelves. We're taken out and thrown in the Old Bill car. The look of joy on their faces was like they'd just nicked the Great Train Robbers.

We get to the station and the sergeant is informed we're both here for breach of bail conditions and we will be held till the morning and then bail will be denied and we'll be off on remand.

We're put in separate cells but don't stop banging on the door and pressing the buzzer and shouting you've fit us up you slippery bastards, my solicitor is going to rip you a new arsehole tomorrow. One of them opens the hatch and with a smirk tells me to keep the noise down.

I eventually fell asleep and am woke by the door opening and the sergeant telling me there was a terrible mistake and we're free to go. What you on about I ask but I don't get a proper response just that it was a mistake shut up and go home. This brings out my stubbornness, no I'm staying here till the morning and going to court and taking this further. I'm now trying to close myself back in my cell and the sergeant is forcing it open like a Monty python sketch. I'm eventually dragged out of the cell and told to sign for my belongings all the while still demanding to be taken back into my cell. Out comes Terry saying Spence shut the fuck up let's just get out of here.

. In fairness to Julie she'd seen us talking to the coppers from the window and when the probation service was informed of what had happened she went straight down the station and gave them what for, explaining she'd seen the two Old Bill point us up towards the shops with their blessing so something obviously wasn't adding up.

THANK YOU, JULIE

Off we go in our little van to Wales dare I say at the taxpayers' expense. Looking back at this as someone who pays tax and my dues each month from my wages I see this in hindsight as a total piss take, but we were hardly likely to knock it back were we.

We cross the Severn Bridge and enter Wales green and pleasant land. We arrive at a little centre in the middle of nowhere with loads of wooden cabins. We're shown ours which is an absolutely stunning place, big fireplace, kitchen and plenty of bunk beds for us all. The three probation officers are next door in their cosy little cabin and we`re all jealous that Phillip and Pete are going to be able to ogle the most delightful Julie. Deep down in our adolescent minds we all thought she secretly had a crush on us but that couldn't have been further from the truth she was simply a genuinely good lady trying to do the best she could for a bunch of misfits.

There was a large moose head on the wall in the cabin so obviously within ten minutes a massive ten skin joint was rolled and placed strategically in its mouth. This was before mobiles and camera phones but we had some cameras, and photos were duly taken. When Peter entered and saw what we'd done he was truly disappointed in us all and, as always, we were sat down and asked what was going on in our minds blah blah. We were made to remove the spliff and as a punishment were taken out horse riding.

Most of us being from London or its outskirts, the nearest we'd come to a horse was either on telly with the Lone Ranger and Tonto or by the local gypsy camps. Fuckin hell we didn't appreciate the size and power of them till we were all given the proverbial leg up. Flying across fields at upwards of twenty miles an hour clinging on for dear life is an exhilarating and frightening feeling but then there's the crashing to earth when the bleeding thing decides to suddenly stop and launch you through the air. Back for a shower and dinner at the cabin before all sneaking round the back to smoke a few joints. Like a scene from a Carry On film with Sid James and Barbara Windsor we're all trying to catch a peek at Julie as she gets out of the shower, but to no avail.

The following morning, we're told we're doing proper canoeing in the rapids and to take notice when everything is explained to us and not act like idiots. We're given a couple of hours' free time to go exploring so we venture into the little shop nestled in among the cabins. Within five minutes we've got inside and we're helping ourselves to the shop's wares, thinking these backwards taffys won't have a clue. We couldn't have been more wrong and these big burly boyos come out of nowhere, grab hold of us and lock the door.

The probation officers had to dig us out of yet another hole. Apologies were made to the angry looking Welshmen and money was passed and yet again we'd got away with another one, though I'm sure the sight of Julie helped. One of us - Wayne - was on probation for a large number of TDA (taking and driving away). He was a compulsive car thief who could hotwire any car in seconds. He never wrecked a car after thieving it or set them alight. He genuinely loved motors and everything about them. He now runs a large number of garages in Kent and for a time was an advisor on safety and security for several high profile companies.

Back then he was just TDA Wayne.

Sitting about two hundred yards from our cabin was a land rover just calling out to Wayne to come and take it. With no encouragement from us needed, Wayne was in and sitting behind the wheel, engine running and calling us all over for a spin round the nearby lake. We clamber in. It's an open back type with room for all twelve of us and off goes Wayne, wheel-spinning in the mud and getting precariously close to the side of the lake. Next second the edge of the bank gives way and we're in the water. We all jump out soaking wet and leg it back to the cabin with the motor slowly disappearing behind us into the lake behind us.

Oddly nothing was ever mentioned to us about the disappearing car. Very strange as we were all waiting for a knock on the cabin knowing us poor English hard working lads would get the blame. But nothing. Yet another one we got away with.

So after two years of fun and games I was signed off by the probation service as, apparently, suitably punished.

To this day I still cannot fathom how this was considered money well spent on the tax payer's behalf. In my opinion it just taught how better to manipulate a system that was falling apart and pandering to the wrong side of the law. But I was hardly likely to stand up and protest was I?

On our return from Wales one of us - Derek - was informed while we were away his father had passed away. Derek was the quietest out of our dirty dozen and this sudden news, which was literally thrown at him as the probation van was being parked, hit him hard. None of us knew how to react towards him and he swiftly vanished off the radar. Within 18 months, even though his mum was constantly on to the authorities that he was in a bad way mentally, and was supposed to be on a round the clock watch, he managed to hang himself in a prison cell. A tragic end to what the rest of us saw as a result of the legal system giving us an easy ride during probation.

Phillip, Peter and the beautiful Julie were lovely people who had our best interests at heart. They tried all they could to steer us in the right direction. They were three top people who did their very best doing a difficult job in a constant battle with youths who were themselves unsure of their place in the world. Wherever they are and whatever they are now doing I'd just like to say thank you for trying. If you could see me now I know you would be proud. And maybe how you treated me had an input in making me turn my life around.

THE BIG C AND ME - PART TWO

The date that door was quietly closed in the clinical diagnostic unit and I was told that I more than likely had cancer was September 3rd 2018.

I had been constantly tired and was back and forward to the doctors but would be fobbed off with excuses and to stop worrying as I was now fifty and should ease up with the exercise. For quite a while I'd been getting up early before my shift in the library and running 4 or 5 miles most days even though I had the onset of arthritis probably enhanced thanks to Jewish Jack's cowboy antics as well as working out in a little home-made gym. I was told by a GP to maybe run every other day and only do two or three miles a time as I was getting on a bit. I was also an ex user of multiple drugs so really should take it easy. What a great answer from a doctor: exercise less and to stop worrying.

After a constant battle with the receptionists I was sent for a blood test and the very next day -15 August -I was sitting in work when my phone rang and *doctors* lights up on the display. I answer and it goes something like hello Mr Spencer we have your blood test back and the doctor would like to chat to you. Wow that's quick, I say, it normally takes a couple of weeks, shall I make an appointment? No if you could come down now the doctor will see you straight away.

Fuckin hell, now I know this is serious. I go straight to my manager and tell her I've had a worrying phone call from the doctors and need to shoot off. No worries Joe best of luck let me know what happens.

I get to the doctors in twenty minutes and he tells me my iron is virtually non-existent. Thank the lord for that I say, I was proper worried. Yes, but we need to find out why you are so lacking in iron as it could be many things but we need to exclude more sinister reasons. Jesus doc you're making me panic again, what do you mean by more sinister? Well it could be many things but I'm going to get you an emergency camera up both ends and some scans. Jesus Christ, I'm thinking, this is the real shit. The old Joseph would've thrown an instant wobbler and stormed out launching a tirade of abuse and probably a chair or two. Okay Doctor, so when and where and how long? I'm putting you on a pathway, he says, and that all this will be completed within 28 days.

I go into a meltdown and make my way home. I wait till Abbie gets home from work before telling her. She always sees the positive in any situation and simply tells me that me worrying was wasting mental energy and that I needed to focus on being as positive as I can.

Prior to this we'd book a late break to the Canary Islands and had been happily preparing for some September sun. My first couple of procedures were to be not long before we were due to fly away and to be honest the thought of a holiday with the dread of this hanging over me was not appealing at all.

First up was a camera down the throat and this, for me, was the most invasive thing of all. It was so difficult to hold the tube down without gagging. I was asked if I'd like to be sedated and, like the idiot I am, I said no. It was awful and the medic said if you look at the screen Joseph you will see your inner workings. Oh my God why I glanced up from my prone position to look I'll never understand, but I did. And that made me react and start pulling on the cable /tube for the camera which was at that time twisting and turning in my inners. I was admonished by the doctor doing the procedure as I'd been told several times before the start that if I had any discomfort to raise my hand slightly and they would slowly remove the camera as to do it suddenly was dangerous due to the small space of the oesophagus and yanking it could cause serious damage.

The doctor stormed out of the room, fuming. A nurse told me it was because if something went wrong it would be on the doctor's record - even if it wasn't his fault. I then had to apologise and literally beg him to start again. After plenty of begging on my part he agreed and said it's just eight minutes, count to 60 in your head 8 times and it'll be over.

Fucking hell, easier said than done. Eight of the longest minutes I've ever had to endure. After what seemed like an eternity he withdrew the camera and informed me that he'd seen nothing untoward but would still need to stick the camera up my backside to check the lower bowel area.

I was sent home and told to drink these sachets of drink they gave me that would clear me out. I'd had bowel problems pretty much my whole life. In the famous summer and drought of 1976 I had the misfortune of becoming impaled on a rusty spiky fence. I was about 7 years old and just enjoying being an innocent young lad in the baking hot days and nights of that glorious summer. Days were spent going from one friend's paddling pool to another and having water fights with hoses and buckets of ice cold water, playing war with bits of wood as a make believe gun, making bows and arrows and playing cowboys and Indians, hide and seek, runouts, off ground touch and even games of kiss chase with all the local girls. We would make a camp or tent out of absolutely anything that we found and an old discarded pram would within minutes be converted into a go kart and we'd be flying down the mostly car-less side streets with the wind in our hair and not a care in the world.

Eventually that summer there was a hosepipe ban and all the keen gardeners were unable to water their flowers and immaculate lawns but, more importantly for us, paddling pools were harder to come by as people were told to inform on neighbours who were seen to flout the rules. Big brother is always watching. So we found a local lake and that became our new pool.

Our parents didn't know where we were swimming as they'd have rightfully been worried shitless so we all lied and told them we were going over the park but instead would meet up and head to the lake. This lake for years became a swimming area for people from miles around, even though the water was absolutely filthy and all sorts of shit and junk were lobbed in there including cars.

At one point in our mid-teens one summer we were all over the lake off our heads on acid annoying the poor blokes who were after a peaceful days fishing. We were launching ourselves into the lake from all directions making a racket when Dee dives in and comes up holding his guts and says lads look at this I think I need to go hospital. He pulls his hand away from his stomach and he has this ginormous L shaped slash in his gut and loads of intestines just sitting in the palm of his hand. In his tripped out mind he's looking at it all just going wow fuck me man look at this shit man. We're all going Dee push it back in mate, so in the filthy water that people piss and shit in and God knows what else he is tucking his guts back inside and laughing like a madman.

Dee ended up in hospital put out under anaesthetic and having a major operation and was in for several days. When we went to visit him, Dee being Dee - who is immune to most drugs of any shape or form and to this day still is - was telling us how good the buzz was when he came round and that anaesthetic would be worth a fortune on the street. Typical Dee. How he does it is beyond me but he's still going strong to this day and hasn't changed a bit. Nothing, and I mean *nothing*, seems to faze him.

I also had another friend - Vincent - who had a less happy experience of being operated on while on LSD. We tried to gate-crash a party in an area off our manor thinking we could take a liberty, and came unstuck big time. A small firm about, twenty or so handed, we thought we were untouchable and turned up at this house party and stormed in, instantly thieving all the drink, skinning up all over the gaff and sniffing lines, being the obnoxious wankers we undoubtedly were. Unbeknown to us, a phone call was made and this other mob turned up, gave us a proper hiding and turfed us out.

Now you'd think we've got a good hiding and so would fuck off. But not us little group of knob ends. A few houses down the road there was a milk crate full of glass milk bottles, this being back in the good old days of the milkman. Many times in the 80s I would be coming home as the milkman was doing his rounds and jump on and chat to him and he'd give me a bottle of freezing cold milk while he made his early hour's delivery.

So we're all bottled up and Scottish Stuart goes up to the door and starts smashing the door with the crate and all hell breaks loose. Out comes the mob that had battered us 15 minutes ago. It's all-out war - us with the milk bottles and them being all tooled up as well. I did say we were stupid, didn't I, and of course once again we get battered and end up chased in all directions. Except for Vincent, who feared no one. He stood there tripping out of his nut going toe to toe against bats and hammers with the milk bottles we'd nicked. Sadly, for Vince, those bottles would be his undoing.

He was held down once he was overpowered and our foes took great delight in carving his face up like a jigsaw puzzle with broken bits of bottle. He was eventually rushed to hospital and was operated on while on acid and never recovered mentally from the attack. For years after he would wander the streets not knowing much about anything just staring and frightening people, what with his carved up face and standing about 6 foot 6 and weighing about 20 stone, Vince looked like a proper scary character, which if I'm being honest he had become.

There was a time I'd stay at Vince's house and he'd stay at mine. We were very close but after his battering he was completely gone and never really came out of the acid trip he had taken that night. We'd often heard of people who'd dropped an acid tab and never recovered like the old story of a bloke who'd dropped bad acid and ended up tripping for years convinced he was an orange and walked around asking people to peel him while he tore at his skin before eventually ending up in an asylum.

I often used to laugh at this story about the bloke who thought he was an orange, but having had a fair few bad experiences on acid I now think it is very probable someone might never come down from a bad one, as you're relying on people you're never likely to meet again not soaking each acid tab too much and giving you a lifetime of horrors and, in the end, a death sentence.

Not everyone was like me selling blank bits of embassy fag boxes as LSD and doing no harm at all. I was simply obtaining money under false pretences but they could hardly report me to the Old Bill could they?

I'd bump into Vince now and again over the years and after a while he honestly had no idea who I was. He would mumble at me for a bit and then I'd disappear. One day I was out jogging and recognised his sister. I stopped and introduced myself and asked how Vince was and she told me he had died of heart failure about five years previous.

Another one lost.

A heart attack isn't an overdose but that acid he took and getting involved that night at the party had a long lasting effect on him which I'm sure contributed to his heart failure.

Back to the summer of 76 . . .

THE BIG C AND ME = PART TWO

The house I grew up in backed onto a dump where all us kids would play each and every day. One time, I was having a kick about with some neighbouring kids, booted the ball over the fence - the rusty spiky kind which we all for some reason had back then.

The little boy who cried wolf was something my doting mum would often recite to me, especially as I always thought it funny to climb on the rusty old fence and pretend to her horror that I was stuck on the spikes.

So off I go over the fence to get the ball. I'm at the top, turn my feet ready to lower myself down and the top of the rusty spikes scrape my arse. I sort of wriggle and next thing I know the rusty spike's gone right in just above my as yet unmanly manhood, piercing me in the lower belly. I scream and yank upwards taking the spike with me till it goes in the bottom and out of the top of my guts. I'm screaming me goolies me goolies which was a new word I'd recently learned. My mum pokes her head out of the back door telling me to stop crying wolf and faints right away as she sees the sight of my white football shorts turning red with blood.

Luckily for me, fate and destiny decided it wasn't my time.

Mavis from next door had at some point had been a nurse and hearing all the commotion comes out and takes control. She talks to me in a soothing voice Joseph stop moving and look at me. Back then in the mid-seventies a mobile was a pipe dream and most houses round here didn't even have a phone so there would generally be a queue at the phone box on the corner which more often than not were broken and stunk of piss and burnt paper where someone had set the phone directories on fire.

Years later I would go around with a crowbar jemmying open these same phone boxes nicking all the coins. Back then we were fortunate that Rene and Arthur the other side had a phone. Mavis tells Renee call an ambulance and tell them you want the fire brigade as well. Renee asks why the fire brigade and Mavis tells her just do as you're told. Arthur's ordered to talk to me and not let me pass out in case I fall off the fence and rip myself to shreds.

He talks to me in his calmest voice about football trying his best to ignore the blood that's gushing out of me. I hear sirens and first up are the firemen who immediately tell me not to be scared but there's going to be a lot of noise just be calm. Mavis holds my hand while the firemen sawed the spike from below and I'm lowered onto the floor of the dump where many times I'd rolled about in the long grass playing hide and seek but this time I've got the life seeping out of me.

The ambulance arrives and I don't remember much else until I woke up with a mess of bandages round my middle. I'd badly punctured my bowel and groin and was very lucky to be alive. I didn't have a biological dad, so to speak, and my step dad never came into my life till a couple of years later, but in my brother-in-law, Len, I had a great man in my life. My poor mum was worried sick but all I kept saying was I want Len. He was and still is a truly great man who I am extraordinarily lucky to call my family.

For the rest of that sweltering summer I was confined to the house like a hermit. I couldn't walk for months and for a good few years couldn't drink anything fizzy or eat certain foods. One good thing to come from my misfortune was that all those ridiculous spiked fences were removed from all the back gardens and replaced with less harmful wooden ones.

Anyway, back to me as an adult and that camera going up where the sun doesn't shine. I drink the sachets the doctor gave me and I have never experienced bowel movements like it. The whole night I'm on the toilet till it feels like there's absolutely nothing left inside me. Next day

I am in hospital and given what the nurse called modesty pants, which are like a black paper type underwear with a hole in the butt for the specialist to gain easy access to my arse. I'm slightly sedated and wheeled to a waiting room full of blokes who had the same procedure. - in truth - it's so much less invasive than the camera down the throat.

The bloke next to me said I'm recovering from bowel cancer and as soon as I'm told it's still clear and I can fart they'll give me a cuppa and a few biscuits and let me go, and you'll be the same mate. Everyone's slowly getting told they can go home and I'm left sitting there farting to myself.

I ask when I can leave and the nurse says the doctor would like to speak to you in private along with your partner. Fuckin hell I'm thinking this is really happening, this is really deep. My arse had been intruded by instruments all day and now it was falling out with fear. I ring Abbie and she asks me if I'm all finished shall I come and get you. I explain they want to speak to us privately and she's there like a shot.

We're taken into a room with a couple of clinical specialists and the man who'd done my procedure. He says he's taken 20 samples from something sinister looking in my lower bowel. I ask is it cancer. Fuck knows how I found the strength to speak as all the strength had gone from my body. I was on autopilot. He informs me he isn't qualified to tell me what it is but they'll send the samples off, and get the results and go from there.

He then says I'm sending you tomorrow for a full body scan to see if it's spread. Your saying that like you are talking about cancer I say to him. Look Mr Spencer I spend my days looking inside people's bowels and I've seen something I really don't like so we're going to get things going as fast as possible.

I somehow got home and fall into a deep and sombre mood, convinced I'm going to die of cancer like two of my beautiful sisters had done. Each time I closed my eyes I'd think fuck fuck I've got cancer I'm going to die and I wasted so many years not caring about life and now I love life it's being snatched away from me.

Next day I'm off to a different hospital for my scan. I have to drink a couple of litres of water and hold it in so that they can see my innards better. As I'm lying on the scanner with the noise thundering like mad around me I'm convinced this is the end. I'm told I'll get a phone call in a couple of days with the results.

Those days were so hard. I was completely selfish and went into myself, shutting Abbie out and everyone else.

A couple of days later I'm called in for the results and given the news that there's something on my liver that will need an intense scan. Fuck I'm dying. This time I have a cannula put in my hand and I'm going to have a blue dye injected into me so they can see what needs to be done. In the side room the nurse put the cannula in my hand and says she'll collect me shortly.

I'm sitting there in my little hospital gown on the verge of breaking down when I catch a glimpse of my notes.

Now up to this point though it's pretty obvious I've got cancer but no-one's actually said it and I haven't seen anything in writing, so in my mind there's the slim hope that little Joseph might somehow obtain a miracle and get out of another mess. But then I see it in my notes. In black and white:

Cancer of the lower bowel, checking liver to see if it has spread.

I burst into tears and rip the cannula out of the back of my hand, blood spurting everywhere, and leave the room just as the nurse is coming in to collect me. Joseph what's happened come let me help you. She was a lovely little Philippine with a gentle calming tone and she dresses my hand and we sit and speak. You knew deep down Joseph you had cancer now let's get in there and see if it has spread, and if it has you will fight it all the way, we can do miracles. Yes, but it's taken two of my sisters this horrid beast of a disease, she simply says well the odds are in your favour

126

then. I go in the scan machine again with a new cannula in the other hand and a couple of stitches in the one I'd pulled the cannula out of. I'm spoken to from another room via a microphone. Breath in Joseph and hold for ten, breathe out Joseph and hold for ten. Well done Joseph you will get your results in about a week.

That week turned into eleven days. Torture like I never knew possible. I was convinced it had spread and started getting things in order. I arranged my funeral from start to finish. Songs and a poem to be read out. This somehow all helped keep my mind in order too. I had two choices. I could give up or fight, plain and simple. Giving up would have been so easy. But I had Taylor, my little granddaughter, who was barely a month old. She had no idea who I was, I had children and Abbie and family who loved me unconditionally. I owed it to them to at least fight this fuckin beast and give it my all.

A mate got in touch and told me about cannabis oil and how good it was for cancer and dropped me a large amount off, but I never touched it, I was going to do this the proper way, though I will not knock anyone fighting this disease in whichever way they choose or whatever means they feel is necessary, but for me it wasn't an option I wanted to take.

The phone finally rings with a withheld number and I know it's the hospital.

THE BIG C AND ME - PART THREE

Hi Joseph we have all your results and the specialist wants to see you as soon as you can get here. After waiting for eleven long days and nights for this I now couldn't face the journey to the hospital to hear the diagnosis. Please just tell me now I pleaded but was told it wasn't her place and the specialist needed to tell me as it would be unethical for her to break protocol. I told her in no way was I mentally able to either get the bus and train or in a cab or ask anyone for a lift for this news as I was emotionally destroyed already. Okay, Joseph it is cancer in your bowel - which deep down you and we knew - but it is just fatty tissue on your liver and definitely not cancer. Wow. In a perverse way that actually made me feel better. She was correct. I knew it was cancer in the bowel and that this is known to have a strong link with liver cancer. But it's not liver cancer. I had a fighting chance. She made me promise to look surprised when the specialist told me the news and, somehow - I don't know how, I stuck to my word.

The consultant explained to me the cancer in my bowel was more than likely stage two and I would be in within the next few weeks to have it removed. I was then given the news I would more than likely be fitted with a colostomy /stoma bag which I would shit into for the rest of my days. Hearing that news was absolutely soul destroying.

Abbie put it in perspective when I said but I'll smell and what will people think. Straight to the point as always, she said you always smell like you've shit yourself when you fart so it'll be nothing new. And if people can't handle it that's their problem and we won't miss them in our lives, whereas those who love you will just be glad you're still here.

Then came the traumatic experience of going to visit the stoma nurse in the stoma room. The shelves were full of bags of all kinds and types. A permanent marker was used to mark both sides of my belly. The nurse told me depending on where I had the bag would depend on which side it was placed on my stomach. On one side would be the type that fills up constantly and the other side would fill up slower, but both would entail me having to change these bags regularly. It really was horrific sitting in that room, but as the old saying goes, shit happens.

My mind set had changed hundred percent and I was determined to be positive for myself and those who loved me - especially my beautiful granddaughter, Taylor. I carried a little photo of her with me to all appointments and kept telling myself she needs her grandad. A few years down the line when she first attempted to say grandad and instead she called me mamad I cried happy tears. Then it became rarad them grangrad then eventually grandad.

Truly special and truly worth fighting for, that's my Taylor.

I was told I'd be in the hospital for at least a week, so packed a small case. The day before the operation I had to once again drink those awful sachets to make me shit through the eye of the proverbial needle. Our holidays we had planned sadly didn't happen as I just couldn't face sitting on a plane and sitting round a swimming pool knowing I had something growing in my body that was trying to kill me, I just couldn't do it. We'd been advised by all the doctors and medics to go as it would apparently do me good before the operation. I went along with what they said right till my nephew Shane turned up in the early hours to take us to the airport. I broke down. Shane sat with me for hours gently talking to me and advising me. That man is a credit to his dad Len and my sister and again I am so proud to be a part of his family and share his DNA.

We ended up losing about fifteen hundred pounds as I had left it too late to cancel. The oncology team wrote a lovely letter on my behalf trying to get me a refund but the travel company and insurers dug their feet in and refused to budge.

But I didn't care. Life and good health are worth so much more than money and I just put it down to experience.

I was determined to travel on public transport as Abbie was due to start a new job on the day of my operation. I insisted she go in as I didn't want to risk her losing it before she'd even started. If I was going to pass away I wanted to be sure she had an income. I'd made sure she had access to my small pension and my online bank details etc. I travelled by bus and train to hospital with my little case of belongings and this journey was even lonelier than a sweat box, but in a different way.

The sweat box is self-inflicted - this was a whole new feeling. I was glancing at strangers wanting to tell them how lucky they were to be doing everyday things and to tell their loved ones how important they are as I'm about to be put out and may never come round. I felt like I was heading to my own execution. I sat there and imagined how my late mum would have reacted to her little Joseph being diagnosed with this disease after it had taken two of her daughters. It would have destroyed her. I owed it to the memory of her to remain positive.

Nothing with me is ever straightforward, though.

I'm given a gown, another cannula is inserted into my hand and my little name tag with name and date of birth is strapped to my hand. I'm given a little pair of red socks with grips on the bottom. What's that all about? I ask. So you don't slip walking to the theatre. You're having me on, I say, I'm walking there? I thought I'm getting put out, laid down and wheeled in? No, you walk and we'll show you the theatre and introduce you to the whole team. Fuck off will you, the whole team, I'm not fucking playing football, I'm thinking.

Half hour later a nurse comes to collect me and off we go.

As we're trudging along she says something along the lines of what do you do for a living Michael? Do what? She starts again and I say what did you call me? Michael something or other she says I point to my wrist and tell her in no uncertain terms my fuckin name is Joseph Spencer. Oh I'm so sorry she says I should have checked before we left your bay. Too fuckin right you should. So off we go back to the bed where in clear letters above it says my name and date of birth.

I often wonder what Michael was in for and would I have woken up with a limb missing or a sex change and become Josephine.

Eventually a different nurse turns up and asks if I'm ready. I've been ready ages but first what's my name? She asks my name and date of birth and I confirm it and tell her of my earlier encounter and she says she'll report it. Normally I wouldn't agree but this was too serious so I said make sure you do cos I intend to. Off we go on my way to being put out but in reality felt like the walk to my death. All I'm thinking is please come round from the anaesthetic and a successful operation.

I stand outside two swing doors and I'm greeted by a nurse who welcomes me like I've arrived at a restaurant. I've no idea what this is about, this way of doing things - whether it's to cut down on staff or something - but it frightened the life out of me. I'd have preferred to stop outside the theatre, lay down and be anaesthetised and then wake up in a recovery room but as I say nothing is ever simple with me. I'm told to sit on the bed and introduced to 'the team'. This is so and so who you've already met who will be doing the actual surgery, this is so and so who will be monitoring all your vital statistics. And I'm just nodding thinking fuck me Jeremy Beadle's going to jump out in a minute. Then they showed me the fuckin tray of blades. Please are you trying to give me a heart attack before you start or what, I once again think to myself. Scalpels of all shapes and sizes sit on an aluminium looking tray. They then tell me to lay down and I have a massive panic attack and my blood pressure drops ridiculously low and someone is talking soothingly in my ear.

Next thing I know I'm waking up in a little bay with blue hospital curtains around me with Abbie holding one hand and my sister Susan holding the other, both of them gazing at their little Joseph with nothing but love. Being loved not for what you are or what you can do or give but just cos of you - is a beautiful feeling. Better than any drug. I am blessed in life and love. My hand travels down to feel the stoma colostomy bag that is to become a part of me and everything I will do.

But I can't find it. It's not there. Where's the bag? The doctor said the surgery was completely successful and you don't need it. Oh my God - or any God - I love you with all my heart. But the doctor is going to advise you on a course of chemotherapy. Even though he has removed all the cancer the chemo will be an added precaution but it's up to you whether to go ahead with it or not. Abbie and Susan had been very worried as it was now about 10 o'clock at night and I'd been gone for hours. They were informed that due to my previous bowel operation in the summer of 76 it had been a difficult procedure but my doctor was brilliant and not only managed everything he had to but also achieved it without the need for stoma.

What a man and what a great team.

Yes, hallelujah.

I'm finally given a room in a ward at about midnight and I'm kissed goodbye by these two special ladies, one who I share my DNA with and the other who simply loves me with every beat of her heart. I understand I am one lucky man. I'm wheeled into a ward with five other blokes who had or were waiting for similar ops, but to be honest I was still smashed from the anaesthetic to take much notice of anything.

I'm asked would I like a sandwich and old silly bollocks here says yes, and I'm given for fuck know what reason after a major stomach operation - a roast beef sandwich.

Within seconds of tucking in I'm throwing it up all over the gaff till the bloke opposite produces a cardboard hat type thing which I fill to the brim with roast beef sandwich vomit. I'm Steve he says and knock me sideways he's ex-CID or Canvey Island Dustmen as we used to call them. We could spot them and their undercover cars a mile off. Steve was in to have a stoma bag reversal. He'd had the same as me a few years ago and had the bag and was now waiting to have it removed, which I've now found out is more common than people know. Though I've since met other cancer survivors who, after having the bag removed, request it to be replaced as they struggle to control their own motions.

Steve was a lovely bloke who gave me great advice over the coming days regarding my cancer and what to expect in the future. We also had the room in fits of laughter talking and telling stories from different sides of the law. He fully understood I was a completely reformed character and told me if I'd chosen another direction I would have made a great copper.

Also in the ward was a bloke in his 60s from Trinidad named Alfred. A lovely bloke who was about 10 stone tops. When he showed us his clothes they were all for a man twice his size. Alfred had been told about a year previously he had cancer of the oesophagus and instead of dealing with it he jumped on a plane back to the Caribbean and spent the next half a year laying on a beach drinking rum whilst being unable to eat. He eventually came back from his life in the sun but by then was very ill and couldn't hold anything down. A doctor comes to his bed, pulls the blue curtain round for privacy and gives Alfred stern abuse for going AWOL. Alfred I could have operated and removed the cancer but by running away it has grown and there is nothing I can do. The doctor pulls the curtain back and storms out of the ward with the rest of us not knowing what to say or where to look.

Alfred had just been given a death sentence in our presence so we all sort of pretended we hadn't heard till he was ready to speak to us. He lay there for a couple of days, blanket pulled right up to his chin not speaking or drinking. It was like he'd given up. Then thank fuck another less brutal doctor turns up and tells him that he could shrink his tumour with radiotherapy and chemotherapy. This was the lift he needed.

I would often bump into Alfred over the coming months when I went up to the oncology department for blood tests and to get my chemo pills signed off, and I noticed he was slowly putting the weight back on. I was so lucky in that I had a chemo called capecitabine - which is in tablet form - four each morning then four each night each for a fortnight and then a week off for the body to recover then start again. This went on for 6 months. I was offered the chemo as an added prevention.

I was sat with one of my saviours a little Iranian man who was a professor of oncology. When he offered the chemo he told me the choice was mine. As far as he could see my cancer was removed completely but as he put it if one cell has gone elsewhere I'd be in trouble so I took his word and went for it.

During my time in and out of hospital I would scribble little verses down and read a couple to the nurses who called the professor out and said listen to this. So before long I had a few uplifting cancer poems up on the walls of the oncology department. I would often sit in there and witness another patient reading something I'd written. Welling up they would say how moving it was. I would inform them it was my verse and we would sit and cuddle. This happened many times, and the bond with others going through the same battle was like nothing I've ever experienced before.

Loved ones can comfort you but only those who have gone through the same mental and physical anguish can truly understand. It's not a club I'd have chosen to be a part of but I am and will always find time to chat to others going through it.

FAREWELL TO THE DUKE

2020 and lockdown is at its peak. The library where I'd been employed for upwards of 18 years was sitting empty and locked with a million words and books just waiting for human life to come back and turn a page.

For a fair few years I'd been speaking publicly and also on occasion reading poems that I'd penned to mostly appreciative audiences whether they wanted to listen or not. I've not felt an urge to get a buzz for many a moon and am more than happy in my little part of the world and knowing my place within it. I fully understand I don't have to impress anyone. I don't have to fit in with anyone or any group. If people like me that's great. If they don't like me, that's great as well. Not everyone can like you. I now grasp that and don't try to make others like me through being the best shoplifter or the one who is capable of taking the most gear and thinking that's what life is all about.

I'd been hosting online chats during lockdown for men with any problem at all and try to help them speak rather than bottle their feelings up. It's a downfall of the male species that unlike women we struggle to reveal our inner feelings and fears. I was more guilty than most in the past of just this and my remedy of dealing with a problem in the past was to get stoned, or drunk, lash out, act like an idiot, pretend that nothing at all could affect me mentally and generally lie to all and sundry but most importantly lie to myself. Now I love to speak and I love to listen and discuss whatever the subject. Wars might be fought on the battlefield but are ended through discussion of some form or other.

Since sorting myself out I had distanced myself from most people who I associated with the previous life that I led. You cannot stop a certain way of living and still be around the people who you lived that way with and many who are still living that way. It is only when you're totally comfortable in the self that has slowly found a way out of the darkness and shadows the person you were meant to be is revealed. And you wonder how different things might have been if you hadn't turned certain corners on life's journey.

During those awful months of lockdown, I was in my element just trying to help others. scampering about delivering bread, milk and groceries and picking up medication for people. This must surely come from my mum as she was exactly the same. Having someone they could chat to virtually was a Godsend for many during that time and I somehow got a quite large online following. A daily laugh and joke is great medicine - especially when we were all shut up in our homes. I put messages out there asking if anyone had family or friends in need of anything and would drop things on doorsteps and be spoken to from behind masks and through windows. I was at times the only human contact many were having and the buzz from seeing others happy is the best feeling out there. I would never accept payment for stuff I bought. The mental gratitude I got from doing good deeds was more than enough. I have a large collection of books and would advertise the books for others to read and then pass on, and in this way became like a walking door to door library.

The one person I truly wish I'd visited more during those times was The Duke.

I saw him once during this time as he hurried past on the other side of the road and he just raised his hand in a wave and hurried off. Even Abbie commented that it wasn't like him not to stop and chat and tell me that he loved me. He did at one time collect half a dozen books from me and we stopped and chatted in the street for half hour but he wasn't his usual enthusiastic self. But so many weren't at that time. It was a totally out of the ordinary experience for us all.

We were all suddenly stuck at home, many on their own or others stuck at home in abusive relationships. Others had habits and addictions to feed, and I'm sure that would have been a really difficult time for anyone who messed about with any form of drug. Thank fuck my drug days were very much in the past.

Though we led very different lives - I might not see The Duke for a couple of months - I could bump into him and within seconds be in hysterics. Since his big stretch in the 90s he'd kept his head down and had become a decent builder. He was always grafting, now without a gun and earning an honest crust. Paving, fencing, all manual labouring he was all over it.

One of the last times I was with him was typical of him and his whole persona. This must have been shortly before Covid turned the world upside down. Something had happened and he ended up with a broken jaw. He went to the hospital on the Sunday and rang me mumbling away, garble garble, mumble mumble. Couldn't understand a word so he sent me a WhatsApp picture. He had a bandage tied in a bow on top of his head going all the way under his chin reminiscent of Tom out of Tom and Jerry when the old lady's smacked him on the head with a broom. They sent The Duke home dressed like that and he went to work on a building site like a cartoon cat the next day. He had to wait about a week to go back and have his jaw reset.

I said I'll pop up the hospital and see you. I walked in the ward and was informed he was in surgery and should be back soon. I'm waiting and informed he's on his way back up. The door opens and there he is just coming round. He sees me and says while dribbling through his new jaw I love you Joe. Within minutes he's sitting up putting his clothes on saying he needs to go down and have a can of beer and a joint. You can't do that I say knowing full well nothing is going to stop him. An orderly walks in and tells him we have to do your blood pressure etc. before you can do anything. I say look just do it cos if you don't he's going to go anyway. So all his vital signs are okay and within minutes he's downstairs smoking a joint and I'm just looking at him with that same weird admiration I've always had for him.

The last time I saw him we were out for a meal and he was there with one of his daughters, but wasn't his usual chatty self - which really wasn't him. That's why I now always check on males if they go a bit quiet. They'll often say they're fine but that more than likely means they're anything but. This was during a break between the two lockdowns we all endured and I just wish he'd told me he was having such dark thoughts.

As I say I speak quite a lot to audiences and have become comfortable in that role. At first I found it quite daunting looking at others looking back at me, but once I could see they are genuinely interested in what I have to say and interact whether online or in person I find it so uplifting.

Anyhow, me and The Duke had a brief chat and went our separate ways. Sadly, that was the last time I ever spoke to or saw him again. He has a large family of children and grandchildren whom he loved with his whole being and they in turn loved him, and still love him, and miss him immensely.

So one week after I see him, I'm standing talking on a stage about men's health. Only about twenty or so people are there but I'm in full flow. I always leave my phone on silent while talking as I find it rude to even look at it while others are listening or talking about themselves.

My phone kept vibrating in my pocket every minute or so and I'm thinking this must be important but I waited till a break before having a look. I had missed calls from The Duke's Mrs and a couple off his kids and messages from other old friends saying *ring me Joe* and *have you heard about Duke?*

I try one number but it's engaged then I try his son. He answered literally sobbing and just said Joe he's done it he's gone. What you mean, who's gone calm down I say but I start shaking like fuck knowing something serious has happened. Then he says Dads hung himself Joe.

I don't remember much else of the call or the rest of the day. I somehow finished up the stage talk, rang Abbie and just burst out crying telling her what had happened. He was a man loved by so many but had no real idea of the love that we felt for him. He could be loud and in your face but he had a massive heart and a massive laugh who lived a massive life. And for whatever reason decided he could go on no more.

Like a lot, I used to nod in agreement when people would comment that when someone takes their own life it is a coward's way out and what about those left behind. Well The Duke had never been a coward in his life and had suffered being bullied as a small kid to serving many years inside eventually spending time in Parkhurst on the Isle of Wight with some of the most dangerous individuals imaginable and had got on with it and was never intimidated or phased. He wrote and told me how he looked out of his cell and would see Reggie Kray or the Black Panther. He even played badminton with Reggie and The Duke said he was fit as a flea and a top player as well as being a top man and would spend time in the prison gym with him.

Parkhurst was a bit like the Alcatraz of the UK, being out on the island. To visit we had to travel to Portsmouth and jump on the ferry. A seriously long day. But I did this many times to visit my old friend. The visit would always end with him telling, me to cheer up and have a beer for him. A very special human being indeed. Yes, he made mistakes - some very big - but he paid his dues for those locked behind walls where another human being holds the key to your freedom and came out a reformed character. For murderers, rapists and child abusers I'm all for throwing away the key but for most other crimes you cannot just lock people up indefinitely, there has to be more education, not just for those inside but also for the general public.

As I said, The Duke came through a number of years in Parkhurst - an A cat nick for the prisoner's other nicks couldn't handle, nothing more than a dumping ground for the most dangerous and violent prisoners in the system. He had falling outs in other nicks and I recall visiting him some gaff or other not long before they shipped him to the island and he was on supervised visits as someone had taken a liberty and The Duke had given him a battering with a large vinegar bottle in the kitchens.

Another time a nick made the mistake of putting The Duke in a cell with an old mate of his from our manor and they ended up barricading themselves in the cell and setting fire to their mattresses. So yes, he caused trouble from time to time, but the system tends to drive people to it.

When The Duke ended up in Parkhurst, all the times I saw him and wrote to him he never complained, he just accepted it. He made it through and came out and got on with life working pretty much every day, though he still liked a drink and a smoke. So the shock that he took his own life came as a bolt from the blue from all who knew him. Sadly, he had no savings and nothing put aside but within a few days we all raised the money for a good send off for a top man.

A friend had seen The Duke walking with a dog lead to somewhere many of us played as kids, swinging the dog lead but with no dog attached. He asked The Duke where the dog was and The Duke just said hello and carried on. He said he seemed fine and not in any way upset. My guess - and it is only that - is he had simply decided for whatever reasons it was time for him to leave this physical world and be at peace. From what could be ascertained he climbed a tree, tied the lead round his neck and decided he couldn't go on no more. He never left a note and his phone had no messages or anything suggesting what he was planning on doing. He did have a great send-off where many funny stories were told and I was honoured and privileged along with his sons to carry The Duke off on his final journey.

His Mrs, children and grandchildren are always in my thoughts, as is he.

Sleep tight my old friend.

THE LONG FIST OF THE LAW

I've had many run-ins with the police constabulary during my life though thankfully now I don't have any at all. I'll tell my granddaughter the police are there to protect you so always be polite and respectful to them.

This obviously wasn't always the case back when I was a little shit. The police were a force but have since become a service. When they were a force you knew there were boundaries you didn't cross and if you did there would be repercussions.

There was a particular copper - proper old school type - who'd rather give you a good hiding than bother nicking you. We'll call him PC Hickmott. I'm sure most towns in the 70s and 80s had a PC Hickmott. Our PC Hickmott would catch you doing something and say right we can go over the dump and have a straightener or I can take you down the station, waste all our time by throwing you in a cell and possibly get nicked.

It was a sort of rites of passage that we would all at some point get a good hiding from PC Hickmott. If you took him up on the offer he would produce a pair of very delicate white gloves like a snooker referee would wear, take off his helmet and coat, roll up his sleeves, stand in a boxer's stance and then it was pretty much a sparring match but without boxing gloves and a gum shield. He would have it with you till you said you'd had enough, then brush himself down, take the gloves off, put his helmet back on, shake your hand and tell you to piss off and behave yourself.

How was that for local policing. None of us would have dared mention what had happened to a parent as we would have been in even more trouble. Back then just his name would instil fear into most right minded people. As you got a bit older you understood he was only doing things the way he thought best and I have to agree with the way he did it.

More than one occasion I made the mistake of going behind the dump with PC Hickmott and would surrender in seconds after he'd rained a few blows in my direction. I was never really much cop at fighting but still preferred a quick jab and hook from Hickmott than being thrown in a cell.

But we all eventually meet our match and one-day PC Hickmott met his.

A young lad by the name of Drew, who'd started off in a Detention Centre for a short sharp shock then was sent for a stint in Borstal, had an encounter with Hickmott which finally ended the myth of invincibility that surrounded our old foe. He offered Drew the usual choice to which Drew had come prepared with his own pair of white gloves and they both disappeared round the dump. After a couple of minutes of the sounds of what we assumed were Hickmotts blows smashing into poor Drew's ribs and jaw, out comes Drew with not a mark on him. He calmly turns to us and says you'd better go and give him a hand. We all rush round and there he is, the great undefeated dragging himself up from the floor, blood coming out of his nose and the onset of two lovely shiners forming round both his eyes. Well, well, well, he says through his bloodied mouth, he's certainly got a good career in the ring in front of him.

Drew shook hands with Hickmott after and told him he'd been top boxer in borstal and was looking at it as a possible way out of a life crime. Sadly, for Drew, it wasn't to be. He became a very good amateur boxer but got involved in an altercation with a pub doorman and with his hands of steel nearly killed the bloke. Shortly after, while on bail, he answered a knock at his door where someone apparently wearing dark clothes with a crash helmet ended Drew's life on the spot with a bullet in the head. No-one was ever charged for the murder and yet another life was over before it had the chance to find its way.

On another occasion I knocked for a mate and Lee, his brother, opens the door, saying Joe you need to have a word with him look what the daft fuckers done. Coming down the stairs was my mate Andy dressed in a copper's black overcoat with all the silver shit on the top of the sleeve and a copper's hat. Not just your run of the mill hat neither but one of them flat inspector types.

What the fuck mate where's that all come from? Old Bill had turned up en masse round the corner and Andy had been walking passed and as they all went running in all directions Andy decided to look in one of the open vans and saw the bounty and thought I'm having that. Now it's one thing to wind up Old bill but for the copper to lose his uniform was a sackable offence, being as in the wrong hands that coat and hat could lead to all sorts. I said you need to put that back, mate, otherwise you'll get some serious bird. Exactly what I've been telling him, Joe, says Lee. It's just a laugh, Andy says, looking at himself in the mirror stood in the copper's uniform, laughing his head off and preparing to roll a joint. Mate you've got to get rid, I says, I ain't having fuck all to do with it and I go to leave.

But as I'm about to open the door I hear the crackle of Old Bill radios. We look out the window and they've given up looking for whatever they were initially on call for and instead were hunting for the uniform. Fuck you mate, I say again, I'm out of here. As I walk out to the gate I'm surrounded by Old Bill and straight away thrown on the floor, questions raining down on me about the uniform etc., to which I'm insisting I ain't got a fuckin clue what you're on about. Andy comes out minus his new attire feigning ignorance and they're on him too saying someone fitting his description blah and we're both thrown in the van. We're told the extreme shit that not only are we in but also the copper who has lost his gear is in also and that he is prepared to go to any lengths to get it back.

We're driven to the Old Bill station and all the while I'm giving Andy daggers. The daft fucker proper fucked up and now I'm being dragged into it. We're given snidey little back handers all the way to the local nick and thrown in separate cells. I ask if I can make a phone call as I may well be able to get the missing uniform returned as long as we can leave here with no questions asked. Old Bill is in full agreement so I'm given the phone and call Lee.

Now growing up many of us had a way of speaking whereby letters were changed at the start and end of each word. It was called diddycoy by some and back slang by others and unless you knew it you were never going to understand what was being said. So I call Lee out of my encyclopaedic book of phone numbers that were stored in my brain back then. No mobiles and nothing was on paper so somehow we all just knew and could recall phone numbers at the drop of a hat.

Nowadays I don't even know my own number.

I tell Lee in back slang to go take the uniform to a bin, call the Old Bill from a phone box and say he's just seen an old tramp dump it in there. The Old Bill wants to know what I've said but I just say I think someone may have found it. Ten minutes later the cell's opened and we're told we can leave with no charge, what with it being all a misunderstanding. There's that slight pattern emerging of Old Bill letting you go when they know they're in the wrong. Yes, Andy was a daft fucker for taking it in the first place but the van shouldn't have been left unlocked.

All's fair in a game of cops and robbers.

Yet another occasion of Old Bill being old school was when a load of Lego had gone missing from a lorry. Now it might sound petty - and probably is - but it was about a grands worth of the stuff. I was due to be going swimming at the local lake with a few mates and was rolling a nice big joint for the journey and was waiting for Lunchbox to turn up as he was waiting on his usual take out snacks before going. I've just finished rolling the joint, the end all twizzled and ready to be ripped off before being lit and it's hanging out of my mouth and in my hand I have my towel and swimming shorts, when there's a knock at the door.

I open to what I'm expecting is Lunchbox but it's a copper. And there I am, straight in his face with the joint clenched in my mouth like a cigar. He calmly tells me he's come to take me to the station for questioning regards the theft of the Lego. He then tells me he's giving me exactly one minute to go back in, close the door behind me and flush the joint down the toilet then he is going to knock and we will start again. Yes, officer, thank you officer. I slam the door run upstairs flush the joint down the bog and he knocks again and true to his word introduces himself and starts all over again.

Seems like I wouldn't be going swimming on this particular sunny day.

I get to the station and there's Lunchbox complaining they'd taken his trademark bag of goodies off him. Even the Old Bill referred to him by his nickname and not Colin. Separate cells again and in and out for questioning where we both deny any knowledge of said Lego. Eventually we're told we're being let go without charge. As I'm shown to the front door of the Old Bill station this copper says Joseph just out of curiosity did you have any of that Lego? Course I didn't. Look, he says, I could have nicked you for that joint but was straight with you, so just off the record did you or didn't you have anything to do with it. Yes, yes I did, I replied. Then he calls me a slippery bastard and tells me to piss off. End of. No repercussions he just accepted that today wasn't his day.

Yet another occasion when Plod was more than fair compared to nowadays when they'd never have allowed what occurred. New year's eve party in the late 80s and I'm passed out in a bedroom at about 2 am with some female lying next to me when I hear is Joe there his house has been burgled. I manage to stagger downstairs, do what? Mate your cousin has burgled you. Oh for fuck sake I knew it was going to happen. Knowing he's a wrong'un my mum and stepdad had still let him stay as they always saw the good in others - even downright wrong'uns like my cousin. My darling cousin is my namesake but for now we'll just call him Joey.

He was a good 15 years my senior had been in and out of different nicks forever. To put it bluntly he was a total waster. For all my skulduggery in my life I've never burgled a house whether that be a rich or poor looking gaff. I'd have nothing to do with anyone involved in that lifestyle and only saw them with contempt. They were stealing from their own. Some would say but no he only burgles rich people? What a total load of bollocks. Just because someone lives in a nice house and has money doesn't give you the right to take their belongings and worse thing of all invade their sanctuary.

Joey had been burgling for years and one of my sisters would often tell me to steer clear of him even if I bumped into him on the street as he was a wanted man. Once, in my early teens, I went along with my aunt and uncle to see Joey in Lewes nick. He was behind protective glass in a single room and told me he was in for armed robbery. He also told me he was segregated for chinning someone. I was completely taken in by his bullshit. I found out a few years later he was in solitary for his own safety.

When my sister told me to avoid him on the streets I thought she meant because he was a naughty villain when in fact he was a petty thief who also happened to be a paid police informant. It turned out he was planning robberies which was referred to as going over the pavement whereby they would rob security vans while delivering or collecting money from banks. He would be in on the planning then sell the information to the flying squad which obviously upset a lot of people. So when he came to stay with us to say I was on edge would be an understatement.

So Joey gets blamed for the burglary of our house. That night he also stole my next door neighbours pride and joy Volkswagen Beetle which then went missing for a couple of days. On his return minus the car which he's already sold Joey denies all involvement in the burglary. I get The Duke, an old mate Ginger Paul, and a couple of others as back up and we give him a proper battering with some proper solid

Champagne bottles left on the street from the New Year's piss-ups. We duly clump him round the head with them a few times and after that thank fuck he disappears claiming his innocence.

A few years later I'm sitting in the local and a proper old mate who I'll call Shaun. Shaun says I don't know how you can drink with him Joe; after what he did. What you on about mate? Ginger Paul, Shaun says, how can you sit here playing cards with him and drinking - he's a wrong un. No mate you're wrong I've known Ginger Paul donkey's years he used to have a bad smack habit but he's sorted now. Yeah but he burgled your house it ain't right Joe. What you on about you idiot, my cousin did that. I turn round and Ginger Paul's standing there with the beer he's just bought me in his hand with a look of sheer guilt on his face. What the fuck is he on about, Ginge mate? Ginger Paul just drops his head and his eyes are looking at the floor and he says sorry Spence I was bang on the gear at the time. You're fuckin winding me up how the fuck was it you? He says well I knew you was at the party and look Joe I know I deserve a hiding you'd better call Terry, Kev and Michael as I did their gaffs as well. Around the same time as mine was burgled within a few weeks so was the above mentioned. Ring them and tell them I'm sorry and I'm prepared to pay the consequences.

Fuck me I'm in total shock for once in his life my cousin had been telling the truth and had taken a new year's bashing for it as well, and ginger Paul had even helped bash him up. This shows the extent an addict will go to. My cousin was currently inside for a string of burglaries he definitely did commit so I'm seeing that hiding as on behalf of those who couldn't get their hands on him. I go to the phone on the pub wall - the old style with the dials - and through memory call first Terry then Kev and Michael.

My first words were guess who burgled our houses? Your fucking wrong'un of a cousin came all three replies'. No, it was Ginger Paul. He's here now in the Partridge and admitted it and wants us to give him a hiding. The response was again the same from all three: keep the piece of shit there. They all arrive and the governor knows what's about to happen and says please lads don't do it in here go round the corner. So we all troop round the corner and Ginger just stands there and says go on kick the fuck out of me.

Bearing in mind I'd known Paul since infant's school and we'd slept over at each other's houses and the morning after I got robbed, before my cousin reappeared, he even came round and knocked on my door to help me look for him.

You've got to give it to him he had some serious front.

So we're all standing there, Ginger with his hands by his sides beckoning us to bash him. No matter what, I just couldn't do it. But when Terry - who was a very decent southpaw - exploded a flurry of punches and Ginger hit the deck - we all start pounding the shit out of him until two Old Bill come running round the corner and stopped us mid-boot and threaten to nick us. Ginger looks up from the floor and through his bashed up teeth and to his eternal credit says I deserve it officer I burgled all their houses. The Old Bill looks from Ginger to us and back to Ginger lying prone on the deck and say, as you were gentlemen, and walk off.

One of the strangest scenarios I've ever been in - and I've been in a few.

Fair play to the Old Bill - that would never happen these days. But they saw it for the street justice it was. To make it even more of a comedy sketch Ginger says just break me fuckin arm and be done with it. So we balance his arm on a kerb and take it in turns to jump on it. He ends up in hospital with a broken arm, broken ribs, and his face smashed to fuck.

Moral of that little episode is things will eventually come back and bite you on the arse. I don't hold any grudge against Ginger. He faced those he had wronged and got his comeuppance.

The last I heard he was back on the gear begging outside Paddington station.

MODERN MIDDLE-AGED JOSEPH

Standing looking at myself in the mirror shaving after the diagnosis, it hits hard. Fuck I've got cancer was all my mind kept saying over and over again. But this isn't my time and I was going to fight it hard with every last breath. My life's different than what it used to be. I have nothing to hide and I talk to the Old Bill on a friendly basis. I do many events and talks with them by my side so we can put across both sides. People, especially youngsters, can hear and I hope actually listen when I talk about the correct way to lead your life but the police have a massive job on their hands. They have to convince youngsters they're not their enemy, that they're not there to incriminate or discriminate but to help. There's a massive gulf between the two sections of society and it needs to be addressed from both sides in order for any real good to prevail.

If I go in a shop now and don't buy anything I feel pangs of guilt that I'm looking suspect and up to no good. But I am simply a middle-aged man, named Joseph to most and Spence to others. A middle-aged man who talks a lot and writes a few blogs and poems and spends his days either working in a library or volunteering.

I know people thieve from shops and sell it on at a ridiculously cheap price like I once did, but now that isn't me. I couldn't and wouldn't nick even a bar of chocolate. It's not my way of life anymore. I've turned full circle.

Since those days I've worked alongside some people who have Down's Syndrome. Once you get to know them you see what they've got isn't a disability but a gift they give to others, that gift being their outlook on life. People who've had a difficult start through no fault of their own - born with disabilities whether that be through missing limbs or speech impediments or anything that is not considered by many to be normal - as far as I've grown to see are very much normal.

Soldiers who've gone off to fight for Queen and country and come back without all they initially went away with, be it legs, arms or mental images they can never shake off. The ones I've met they don't let things stand in their way and they don't complain. They've shown me how beautiful life is. These are the people I now understand are the ones I should've been looking up to years ago.

This reminds me of a fella I knew called Dougie. He was a teenage gymnast who was on the verge of representing GB not just in gymnastics but also on the trampoline. Dougie had the lot. He was fit and had the body and looks that had all the local girls swooning. But then he got into heroin and soon became an addict. Within a few months his looks had gone and his gymnastic body was no more. He was in and out of nick and whilst there he got off the gear and worked out in the gym and would do somersaults and floor routines for money off both the screws and other cons.

A few days before his release he was paid to do some gymnastic move, landed awkwardly and never walked again. He was confined to a wheelchair - which could have sent him down and back on the gear - but instead he got into wheelchair racing. He did marathons and became a top racer in his own right. There was one time I went to see The Rolling Stones at Wembley and Dougie was there with a big crowd of us. None of us had tickets and were planning on buying them from touts outside.

As we got closer to the stadium he said Joe I know how we can blag it in for nothing. Go on mate how's that then. His plan was for me to push him into a crowd of coppers accuse him of losing the tickets and basically call him all the names under the sun. I can't do that Doug mate but he said fuck sake mate I know you won't mean it just look convincing and we'll be in. So I do as he says and push him into a crowd of Old Bill and say he's a useless this and that. Whoa sir says one of the coppers, what you being like that for? Doug pipes up looking all sad and vulnerable and says he's right I am useless I insisted on holding the tickets and someone snatched them out my hand and now we can't get in. Don't you worry sir come this way. I push Doug towards an entrance and he is looking up at me with the saddest face but I can tell he's thinking I fuckin told you and they open the door and we're in Wembley for nothing. we're told Doug isn't allowed on the pitch in his wheelchair and has to go in the disabled section, which neither of us are happy about. But you can't have everything, can you.

The others eventually appear and we leave Doug rocking away in his chair and we all have a great time.

As we're wheeling Doug towards the station a couple of very good looking Canadian girls had taken a shine to him. We got to the stairs in the station we got to lift him but these two girls push in front of us and Dougie tells us all to piss off with his eyes. He spends the night in a hotel living every red-blooded male's dream, and good luck to him. Dougie lived his life as a happy go lucky man and never let the wheelchair become an impediment.

Sadly, a few years on Dougie developed septicaemia and passed away. He never once complained. Another one gone far too soon.

I owe so many people thanks for their encouragement. Little Joe Scotland, Andy H, Garry A - all people who at some point in my life were there for me when I needed them for advice or a chat.

Now, if I'm not working in one form or other, I like to sit and eat with good people. I'll go for a big old fry up with a fella I refer to as Grandad Belly and we'll sit and eat and laugh. Or I'll meet up with Moany Tony who you can probably gather loves a good moan. His son is another who is testament to not letting a disability stop him. Chaz was born with cerebral palsy but has recently just passed to become a personal trainer - even though he only has the use of one arm. I've got a mate - Danny - who I'll spend time playing guitar with and making a racket and Paul who I refer to as six egg Paul as he makes me the biggest omelettes known to man.

I've got an old friend known to all as Boots who was only a year ago at death's door after a random unprovoked attack. He was so badly assaulted he had a heart attack at the scene and suffered a double fracture of the skull as well as bleeds on the brain. The night of the incident his wife rang me asking where he was and I told her I left him hours ago. We ended up being rushed by Old Bill under flashing blue lights to see him. It was an awful sight seeing him already in a coma blood coming from every orifice. This was during Covid and his poor wife was told she was only going to be allowed another visit if it was to say goodbye.

On the Wednesday she got the call that his oxygen levels had dropped badly and his lungs were failing and to come and see him with his children. I travelled down with them and it was one of the worst journeys ever sitting with his loved ones. I wasn't allowed in as it was just family. They'd learned through Covid patients that laying people on their front was a last resort to get the lungs and oxygen flows back in working order, and this what they'd done to Boots. Lo and behold within a couple of weeks he was up and walking about and is now back home. Not fully fit but he'll get there though he remembers nothing of the attack that originally put him in hospital.

Which is a good thing.

Boots has always been a grafter. He's never done any harm to anyone. It was awful what happened to him but he lived to tell the tale. It wasn't his time.

I am so glad he pulled through.

MUM

By 2010 Abbie and myself had moved in to help look after my mum as her disabilities had got really bad. She'd developed a terrible curvature of the spine brought on by spondylitis as well as having arthritis and a hiatus hernia. Life had slowly caught up with her. But she never ever complained even when she had to be pushed around in a wheelchair.

Life had gone full circle and now it was my turn to repay all the sacrifice she had made for me by aiding her as best I could. I would never have been able to do it without Abbie. She had become like another daughter to my mum and would shower her, wash and dry her and cook dinners for her. I understand how lucky I am to have always had women around me who had a massive heart.

And through it all, to my mum I was always her little Joseph.

Early 2016 on a Sunday morning mum was sitting in her chair when she said I think you better call me an ambulance. Now for her to say that was completely out of the blue. She hated going to the hospital. Once, she was so frail she sneezed and broke a bone in her back and even then we still had a fight to get her to hospital. They somehow missed the broken bone for months till I forced them to do an x-ray when it was discovered.

Her whole life had been spent helping others. She was a totally selfless person who always thought of others and never herself.

So she's asking us to call an ambulance and within ten minutes it's here. They do a quick test and inform us all to our shock that she's had a heart attack. They take her in and after a few tests we're informed the heart attack is a mild one but she would need stents put in.

Mum waited for over 8 months for the operation and never once complained even though the heart attack had restricted her movement even worse than usual. Most of her time was spent indoors and when she did venture out it would be in the wheelchair.

Abbie and myself had arranged to travel to the Canary Islands in the September. A few weeks before we were due to go my mum finally got the appointment for her stents, but it fell on the day we were due to fly abroad. No matter how much we tried to tell her we could cancel she insisted we go as it was only for a long weekend and my sister was going with her to the hospital and we had been assured that the procedure was something done each day of the week.

So off we go and on the day we travel, the day of her operation, I receive a lovely voice message from my mum telling me not to worry and to have a lovely time.

By then, Mum was so frail - probably about 6 and half stone - due to the heart attack making her lose her appetite. No matter what Abbie cooked her she could barely eat a couple of mouthfuls and was on liquid feeds from the chemist.

When we finally landed in the Canary Islands and got mobile reception I saw I had so many missed calls from my sister as well as a voice message to call her. I get through and she gives me the devastating news that during mum's procedure the Dr had pierced her aorta. She said Mum had died on the table but after quite some time of trying they had managed to bring her back round.

So back home we go.

And when we get there the lady who for me was the strongest person I'd ever encountered was as weak as a kitten, but still not prepared to give up. During the battle to revive her they broke her ribs. They also managed to lose her set of bottom false teeth which seemed to upset her more than anything.

But she'd made it out of hospital and we had her back and forwards to the doctors and, more importantly to Mum, the dentist to get a new set of Gnasher's. When she got them fitted she was the happiest I'd seen her in an age and slowly regained her appetite. However, the amount of time that she had stopped breathing in the hospital had the effect of making her forgetful of the pain she was in.

Mum had always loved doing crosswords and word searches but I noticed she'd been thinking she was doing them but in fact was just inserting random letters. Either she truly thought she was still doing her quizzes or she was hoping I wouldn't notice she was slowly losing the ability to use her brain correctly.

She was rushed to hospital in the November on a Wednesday, and each day I would visit her and sit and chat to her but I could see she was slowly giving up.

On the Saturday morning she rang me and insisted that I didn't need to come that day as she was fine and I should take a rest as she said it was wearing me out. I agreed but fully intended on going up there that afternoon. We chatted for about half hour before she said promise me you'll rest up today, and that was it. About half hour later I get a call from the hospital explaining she was slipping away and to get there as soon as possible. I rang my sister and we rush to be at her side but she'd already gone. She looked so at peace after so much pain. Due to her curvature of the spine she hadn't been able to lay on her back for many years so I lowered the bed and let her finally lie flat.

Mum's funeral was huge for someone of her age. There were people of all ages present, not my friends but her friends, many much younger than me. I knew she was popular but it was then I fully grasped how well loved she was. Mum could fit in at any setting or environment. Whether young or old she could hold her own. There were friends of Mum there in their teens who she'd helped and nurtured.

As we pulled in to the crematorium the Borough Standards were being held in her honour which I found out is usually only for high ranking dignitaries.

What an honour for a daughter of a Russian Jewish immigrant to have bestowed upon her. My nephew Shane read a most moving eulogy which had us all laughing tears of amazement at this grand old girl.

I could talk about this gentle lady that I had the privilege to call my mum all day, but here I will leave her at peace.

I am now a member of a group created by an ex-fire man that is there to help others. Pure and simple. The group promotes local businesses, has trained councillors, others who can help with money problems, donates to local causes that are close to us all, whether in Kent, London or Essex. It has even helped others to gain employment. I get envelopes posted anonymously through my door with literally hundreds of pounds in shopping vouchers on which is simply written Joseph I will leave it to your discretion to see that these vouchers find their way to those in need. I find it such an uplifting feeling and such an honour to be entrusted in this way and love going out and paying vouchers on to young parents or old people who are struggling.

On occasion I will stand in a shop and spot an elderly person shopping and when they get to the till pay for their shopping with the vouchers. The look of genuine gratitude is such an all-encompassing feeling. My mum did this for decades. That is why she was loved by so many. I've only been in the being kind and helpful game for about 15 years. Compared to my mum I'm nothing but a newbie.

When my time finally comes I will not get a send-off as grand as my doting mother. And I don't deserve to. All I want is for others to say that I did what was right and that I did my best.

But more than anything I hope my mum will be looking down and can finally say, now that is my little Joseph.

God bless x

MY MUM MY HERO

Never meet your heroes
I've often heard it said
Mine used to kiss my cheek
And tuck me into bed

My hero was in my corner
And always by my side
She may not have had great riches
But always managed to provide

My hero held my hand
When I faced my fears
Made me smile once more
And wiped away my tears

My hero cleaned my wounds
My physical and mental scars
Now she shines above me
Among the nightly stars

My hero now has wings
I now speak to her in prayer
When I call her name
I know she is still there

My hero had to leave
To sit with the great and good
I'd love to kiss her cheek
If I only could

My hero gave me life
She carried me inside and out
One day her wings will carry me again
Of this I have no doubt

My hero wasn't famous
Though people knew her name
My hero was my mother
That is my claim to fame

The End?
Or a new beginning?

Printed in Great Britain
by Amazon

43080298R00092